Mental Health Assessments

Living with Serious Mental Illness series

Getting Into the System
Living with Serious Mental Illness
Gwen Howe
ISBN 1 85302 457 0
Living with Serious Mental Illness 1

of related interest

Working with Schizophrenia
A Needs Based Approach
Gwen Howe
ISBN 1 85302 242 X

LIVING WITH SERIOUS MENTAL ILLNESS 2

Mental Health Assessments

Gwen Howe

Jessica Kingsley Publishers
London and Philadelphia

This edition first published in the United Kingdom in 1999 by
Jessica Kingsley Publishers Ltd,
116 Pentonville Road,
London N1 9JB,
England
and
325 Chestnut Street,
Philadelphia, PA 19106, USA.

www.jkp.com

Second impression 1999

Copyright © 1999 Gwen Howe

ISBN 1-85302-458-9

Library of Congress Cataloging in Publication Data
A CIP catalogue record for this book is available from the Library of Congress

British Library Cataloguing in Publication Data
A CIP catalogue record for this book is available from the British Library

Printed and Bound in Great Britain by
Athenaeum Press, Gateshead, Tyne and Wear

Contents

PREFACE   7

1. Mental health assessments: an introduction   13

2. Slipping out of the system   18

3. A 'least restrictive' practice   36

4. The role of medication in acute psychosis   52

5. Slipping into the wrong system   71

6. Carers and a need for caring   88

7. A reluctance to use the law?   109

8. Mental health assessments: summing up   132

GLOSSARY   141
FURTHER READING   145
USEFUL ADDRESSES   147
SUBJECT INDEX   149
NAME INDEX   152

This book is dedicated to Mary Cox, ASW, whose idea it was – when she was responsible for mental health training – that some of us should consider what we would most want her professional colleagues to know and understand about living with a serious mental illness. This in turn led to the birth of this series and, in particular, to the writing of *Mental Health Assessments.*

A note on royalties
Forty per cent of any royalties from this book will be shared between the Manic Depression Fellowship and a local group of the National Schizophrenia Fellowship.

Preface

At a time when those who work with serious mental illness are being encouraged to listen more keenly to sufferers and carers, the *Living with Serious Mental Illness* series provides an impressive opportunity for the consumer to speak and to be heard.

About the series

Each of the books in this series focuses on a different aspect of the the mental health services, with the aim of contributing to a better understanding of the experiences and needs of those having to rely on the present system. A group of carers and sufferers have met together to select case studies known to them and to analyse and discuss these. They have brought with them their own individual experiences and expertize to highlight some of the problems which can make it difficult to obtain appropriate help at the right time. By doing this, they believe that this series will enable students to appreciate at an early stage the crucial issues which influence whether or not a sufferer survives to enjoy a reasonable quality of life, and provide an opportunity for professionals to take a fresh look at and perhaps reconsider their own practice in the light of the experiences discussed.

As the author, I am writing this series with, and on behalf of, an Essex-based pressure group of consumers. Its name – the LEAP group – stands for living with the experience of acute psychosis.

About the LEAP group

At the time of writing, the group is made up of twelve members. Of these, five have personal experience of manic depression (MD) or schizophrenia. The others are close relatives of a sufferer and one of these relatives has also suffered with a depressive illness.

More about the group's members

As a matter of interest, members of the group, whose ages range from 33 to 67 years, come from very diverse backgrounds and, to a quite remarkable extent, they represent virtually the whole gamut of income levels throughout our society. Four of the group have honours degrees to their credit and one has a recent masters degree. One member runs her own business, having previously been a director of an old established London firm, while two regard themselves as 'ordinary housewives and mothers', despite holding down part-time jobs, supporting a mentally ill relative and doing regular voluntary work in their spare time! Two of those members who have survived a psychotic illness have responsible managerial jobs, three have experience of working with the seriously mentally ill and one of these is a trained mental health professional. Finally, all five have been been involved to a greater or lesser extent in speaking in public about their experiences and most of the carers have taken part in professionals' training programmes.

The role of the group

In each book, LEAP group is responsible for providing the input which appears under the headings GROUP'S ANALYSIS and THE WIDER PERSPECTIVE and this is collected in the following ways:

1. by members completing questionnaires sent out with each draft case study, while adding as much comment and information as they feel to be relevant.

2. from discussion at regular group meetings, each dedicated to a particular case study.

On average, during the compiling of the first two books of the series, two thirds of the group's members have attended the meetings (with all members attending at least two of them) and three quarters of the members have regularly completed questionnaires on case studies.

In addition, the contract between members of the group and myself allows for the group's Chair, who has personal experience of a serious mental illness, and at least one other member to read and edit each chapter and a further member to read and edit the complete book prior to its going to the publisher. It also allows for any member of the group to read and comment on any chapter at any time.

The structure of each book

Each book has a similar format. The first and last chapters take the form of an **introduction** and a **summing up** by myself. The intervening chapters focus on separate case studies, each dealing with one aspect of one individual's experience of 'the system'. The last of these chapters is devoted to five shorter case studies to broaden the scope of the experience covered in each book.

The structure of each of the chapters focusing on a case study

These chapters are made up of a **case study** and a short **comment** which includes a pause for thought and an informal exercise. This is followed by the **group's analysis of the case study** and its discussion of **the wider perspective**. The chapter ends with a short **summing up**, relevant **information** and an **exercise**.

Under the heading **comment**, it has been assumed that readers may be interested in critically examining what is happening in individual case studies, perhaps with the help of an informal exercise, before going on to read LEAP group's findings. This could be achieved within a group training context or, equally well, by working on one's own and making appropriate notes before proceeding with the rest of the chapter.

Under the heading **information**, references and extra information are provided which tie up with matters highlighted in LEAP Group's analysis and further discussion. There may be some repetition under this heading, to save the need for cross referencing and so ensure that each chapter is complete in itself for training purposes.

Under the heading exercise, a project is proposed which is suitable for use in a group training context or as a formal piece of written work.

Case studies

The subject of each case study may be a member of LEAP group, or a relative, friend or acquaintance of a member. Importantly, group members come from several different geographical areas and members are involved nationally and regionally in the voluntary sector. Thus case studies are drawn from a nationwide sample. Because of this diverse experience within the group, we are assured that consumers can have remarkably similar experiences throughout England and Wales.

Please note that names and other details which are irrelevant to the basic facts of each case have been changed to protect the identity of sufferers (whether or not they are happy to 'go public'), their families and involved service providers.

What's in a name?

As I have mentioned in introductions to my previous books, it a problem for an author to know how best to refer to individuals who have to cope with the condition which is the subject of their book and also how to refer to those most involved with these individuals. For some, this is an important issue but it is also one on which there is little agreement. Until this situation resolves itself, I hope readers will continue to bear with me while I use the terms 'sufferers' and 'carers' in the interests of expediency and a readable writing style.

Members of LEAP Group have had similar difficulties deciding what to call themselves for the purposes of this series. Several of those who might in other circumstances be labelled with the fashionable word 'user' were adamantly against this and, in the context of their involvement in this series, there was little enthusiasm for the word 'sufferer' either. They eventually settled for the word 'survivor', acknowledging that lots of individuals like themselves are fortunate enough to find ways of largely coping with, and surviving, a serious mental illness.

Similarly, those members of the group who are relatives of individuals having to cope with a serious mental illness were not too sure about the word 'carer' as they not only feel that the word is abused by the system, they also find it rather patronising. In the event, and like others before them, they nevertheless opted for the term 'carer' for the sake of convenience and clarity and nothing better coming to mind.

A message for professionals working with serious mental illness

LEAP group members have asked me to point out that as they are campaigning for better services for everyone who has to cope with a psychotic illness, it is essential that they highlight where things go wrong. They would not wish this in any way to detract from the splendid work of some caring and dedicated professionals out there whose untiring efforts enable sufferers to successfully get on with their lives. LEAP group suspects that these professionals are the same ones who will be most interested in reading a series like this although it does not allow for more than a passing comment on their invaluable contribution to a deserving, but neglected, cause. The group would like to take this opportunity of saying a special 'thank you' on behalf of those sufferers who have received the sort of treatment and care which has freed them to get on with the rest of their lives despite a serious mental illness.

Finally, members of LEAP group may be available occasionally to take part in training programmes for professionals and other mental health workers. Enquiries should be sent to me, with SAE please, care of our publishers.

Gwen Howe, January 1998

CHAPTER I

Mental health assessments
An introduction

Serious mental illness is the name we give to conditions such as manic depression (MD) and schizophrenia. We use the word 'serious', since, although sufferers can be relatively well much of the time, if they have a relapse they can lose touch with reality. This is called a *psychotic* episode. Psychosis is dangerous because sufferers are no longer able to understand what is happening around them and often have no awareness that they are ill and in need of help. At this point, often terrified and paranoid, it is vital that they are protected from themselves and from any immediate dangers. In particular, they need protecting from the ravages of an untreated psychosis, which can inflict irreversible damage on their health and, at worst, lead into an intractable and severely disabling chronic illness.

This book is all about how we can protect sufferers at this point, about the provision the system has made for helping sufferers once they have lost touch with reality and don't understand they are ill and in need of help. It is also about what can happen to these individuals if help is not made available at this time.

A critical period

Usually, sufferers are aware that something is very wrong just before the psychosis sets in. Because of this, they will accept help – even actively seek it – while this awareness remains. This period of awareness, the *critical period,* may last from a few hours to, perhaps, a few days. Sadly, the system is not yet geared into providing such a speedy response. For example, a sufferer or carer may seek help from a mental health worker

– perhaps a community psychiatric nurse (CPN) – who may immediately realize that all that is needed is a little extra medication to tide the individual over a vulnerable phase. The nurse then has to locate the sufferer's psychiatrist and obtain that doctor's permission to authorize an increase in medication. The prescription then has to be obtained. This may all take hours or it may, and frequently does, take a lot longer than that. This means that all too often the sufferer may have lost touch with reality and no longer be prepared to accept help by the time it is made available.

Increasingly, carers put pressure on the system immediately they realize a sufferer is relapsing because they know to their cost that the alternative to obtaining help at this time may be to wait for days, weeks, months – even longer – for the then inevitable crisis with all its attendant dangers. It is now widely acknowledged that untreated psychotic symptoms are bad news; not only for the sufferer's mental health (which may suffer irreversible damage) but also for any career prospects and important relationships – in fact, for everything that's important to most of the rest of us as well as to sufferers.

Meanwhile, we have no antidote to a psychotic episode other than prescribing antipsychotic medication. If the psychosis is left untreated, the quantity of drugs required to control it can vary from, initially, a small increase of the sufferer's normal dose right through to truly enormous amounts by the time that crisis point is reached. Even this will not be adequate if the individual's usual drug has become ineffective after a long period of having no treatment.

What can we do to protect sufferers from their illness?

Once the critical period has passed and the psychosis sets in, then the Mental Health Act 1983 becomes the only real tool with which we can protect sufferers from the destructive effects of an untreated psychosis.

The Act allows for someone with a serious mental illness (or suspected of having such a condition) to be compulsorily admitted to hospital for assessment or for treatment, or, as is often the case, for both. There are three grounds for such an admission:

- it is in the interests of the patient's health
- it is in the interests of the patient's safety

- it is for the protection of other people.

If one of these grounds is satisfied and the sufferer needs to be in hospital for assessment and/or treatment to be provided, then they can be admitted under the Act. So, how do we go about using the law in this way?

Mental health assessments

These assessments are set up by approved social workers (ASWs), that is, social workers who have reached an agreed standard of knowledge about the mental health legislation and mental illness after at least 70 days additional and specialist training.

A mental health assessment usually also involves two doctors, at least one of whom will be qualified to work with the mental health legislation. Each will assess the sufferer's need to be admitted to hospital and if they feel it appropriate they will make their recommendations for this on the appropriate sectioning papers. The procedure for admitting someone to hospital is known as *sectioning* and, once the ASW has these recommendations, it is that professional's responsibility to decide whether or not to go ahead and apply for the admission, usually under either Section 2 or Section 3 of the Act. The first allows for the individual to be detained in hospital for up to 28 days, primarily for assessment, to be followed by treatment if, and as, appropriate. The second allows for the individual to be detained in hospital for up to six months for treatment of a recognized illness. Either section can be discharged at any time that the supervising psychiatrist feels the patient is well enough for this.

In deciding whether or not the sufferer is to be sectioned, the ASW should interview the individual and collate and consider information on their previous medical history, their present situation, the opinions of those closest to them and the opinion of any professional who may be involved with them. If the ASW declines to make this application, despite the fact that doctors are recommending it, then the sufferer's nearest relative (as defined in the Act; see Chapter 2) can be the alternative applicant. However, this option will in most cases depend on the ASW fulfilling a duty to inform the relative of this right and giving guidance on their proceeding with the application.

Current use of the law

It might be assumed, then, that mental health assessments lead to the use of the law to protect sufferers from unnecessary damage. Sadly, this is not often the case. There is a widespread misconception amongst health professionals (see the Foreword of the Code of Practice, *Mental Health Act 1983* for confirmation of this) that sufferers must have reached a point in their illness where they can be seen to be a risk to the safety of themselves or others before the law should be used. In other words, the first ground for admission to hospital catered for in the Act and listed above – that is, 'in the interests of the patient's health' is not usually interpreted as a means of stopping further deterioration and all the risks involved in this. It is not at all unusual to hear professionals explaining to families and friends that the sufferer is 'not sectionable yet'. They are waiting for something to happen – with all the risks this entails – when this is not required by the law.

It seems that many health professionals see this as a civil liberties issue; that it would be abusing the right of a sufferer to detain them before things became so desperate that there was no alternative but to do so. However, this argument does not allow for consideration of other rights that most of us would see as being important, for example, the right to be relieved from torturous symptoms, the right to be spared irreversible damage and the right to be well. Can it be that all of these rights should be sacrificed in the interest of just delaying a period of detention?

An abuse of the law?

It could be argued that to use the law selectively in this way – opting for one ground for admission and ignoring another – is to abuse it. All too often, it seems to families and friends of sufferers that the law is actually used as a justification for *taking no action at all*. Nothing will help the sufferer once the psychosis has taken over until such time as anti-psychotic drugs are prescribed and start to control the symptoms of the illness. As sufferers are not going to agree to take medication on a voluntary basis – *because they do not believe they are ill* – nothing is going to happen to resolve the crisis until they are sectioned and admitted to hospital.

This, in effect, means that during the worst phases of a serious mental illness, those who share the sufferer's life can do nothing but watch the torment and share the pain, the misery and the hostility provoked by paranoid delusions until the nightmare reaches the point when the rest of the world can no longer ignore it! Sufferers and their families are fortunate indeed if they come through this sort of experience undamaged. Relatives and friends who talk of having been to hell and back also sometimes refer to the professionals involved as 'bystanders' or, even 'the enemy'. This sort of reaction can be better understood, perhaps, when they explain that watching professionals turn away without intervening to help a psychotic relative is like watching doctors walk away from an accident where someone you love is urgently in need of treatment.

Mental health assessments which don't take place

Although this is book is entitled *Mental Health Assessments*, it should be mentioned that it is not just concerned with actual assessments; it is also concerned with the frequent occurrence of a missed opportunity to seek an assessment in the first place. In a way, therefore, some parts of the book are possibly as much about mental health assessments which don't take place as about those which do!

Another way forward?

The book is also about the experiences and opinions of some of those who have to cope with psychotic illness either as a sufferer or as a member of a sufferer's family. Because their future welfare depends on us all finding the right answers, they have more reason than most to pinpoint what goes wrong and what changes need to be made. Members of the LEAP group hope that the case studies in the following chapters, together with some of their own experiences and comments, might contribute towards everyone involved with serious mental illness finding a more positive way forward.

CHAPTER 2

Slipping out of the system

Sometimes, professionals working with the mental health legislation assume that a sufferer has to exhibit 'mad behaviour' during a mental health assessment – often a short one-off interview – before being sectionable under the Mental Health Act. Yet it is widely recognized that, when they are psychotic and under pressure, sufferers can become lucid enough to deceive the most seasoned interviewer for up to an hour or more. The following study demonstrates what this can mean for individuals like Kim and for those closest to them.

CASE STUDY

It was a relief to Kim's widowed mother when the young woman returned to her home town shortly after she and her boyfriend split up. For some time her mother had feared that Kim might be very vulnerable. She herself had a tendency to be depressive and her late husband had been schizophrenic for most of his adult life. She had feared the worst since Kim's second year away when she had let on at one point that she smoked cannabis at college 'to help with the times when everything seems black', but she had not been prepared to discuss this further with her mother.

Now she was home again, her mother quickly learned that Kim had again been using street drugs recently, 'when things were going wrong with me and Tony', but she couldn't afford to support the habit any longer. Her mother didn't know if that was why her daughter was having horrendous nightmares and night terrors. She also talked to herself in her bedroom, seemingly ranting and raving at the walls. At other times, her mother would hear her sobbing. She pleaded with Kim to seek help from a doctor rather than go back on to street drugs again. Eventually, Kim agreed to go and see her mother's new GP and to register with him. She told the doctor that she had felt suicidal since she had split up with her partner, but she didn't talk about abusing drugs. The doctor listened and prescribed anti-depressants for his new patient and told her to come back and see him in a month's time. In the event, within a week or so of starting on the tablets, Kim was running amok, claiming that she was being chased by a gang of murderers 'who have got my number!'

When the GP saw the state Kim was in, he asked Social Services to arrange a mental health assessment and by the time that an approved social worker (ASW) and psychiatrist turned up, there was no question in anyone's mind that Kim needed to be in hospital. She was admitted to hospital an hour or so later on a Section 2 (a 28-day section allowing for assessment and treatment as necessary).

By the time she was discharged a month later, Kim had been stabilized on neuroleptic medication which clearly suited her and had been advised to keep taking this. Her mother had explained to the doctors about her late husband's illness and also about Kim's 'on and off' drug habit. The young woman was told that she had suffered a mild psychotic breakdown and that she almost certainly had a similar illness to her late father. It was also explained to her that there was no reason why she shouldn't keep well on the prescribed medication, so long as she avoided taking street drugs like cannabis.

Kim did really well for several months until she suddenly decided to come off her medication because, as she told her mother, 'I'm OK now, not even depressed'. Her mother tried to persuade her daughter to first discuss this with the GP or with the psychiatrist at her next out-patient appointment. However, Kim was adamant and refused to have anything more to do with either doctor. Very soon, her behaviour became bizarre again and there were times when her sudden tempers and verbal abuse quite frightened her mother. In her daughter's quieter moments, she begged Kim to go back on her medication and sometimes she'd agree to do this, hugging her mother and telling her not to worry. The older woman would relax for a few days but then Kim would storm into the house, hostile and aggressive once more.

Before long Kim acknowledged that she was taking cannabis again and she seemed to delight in telling her mother that these were 'pure drugs and not the polluted rubbish the doctors dish out'. Her mother told the GP what was happening and how her home life was turning into a nightmare and she also asked the psychiatrist who had supervised Kim's treatment in hospital to intervene. She was at a loss to understand why both doctors said they could do nothing, but it seemed that this was because Kim herself wasn't prepared to seek their help and there was, anyway, they told the mother, no real emergency. Meanwhile, the young woman continued to abuse drugs and later she became so threatening to her mother that the latter was sometimes too scared to stay in her own home. Even then, she still could not get the doctors to intervene until Kim suddenly erupted about two months later, going quite berserk as she had before her first stay in hospital. Once again, she was screaming and throwing things by the time the ASW and two doctors were available to assess her and they had no hesitation in admitting Kim to hospital under Section 3 of the Mental Health Act, allowing for treatment and up to six months in hospital for an individual who is known to suffer with a serious mental illness.

Kim remained in hospital for about 15 weeks and was stabilized on a depot-injection. Before she left hospital, a social worker found her lodgings with a landlord who was known to be tolerant and supportive. Kim's mother, who had become depressed herself during the traumatic months before the young woman's admission to hospital, felt unable to cope with her at home any longer. On discharge, Kim was assigned a community psychiatric nurse (CPN) to keep an eye on her as well as to administer her injections.

The change in Kim now was evident for all to see. She started attending a 'drop-in' centre quite frequently, signed on for a part-time course at the local college and co-operated with her mother's wishes, visiting her no more than a couple of times a week, when the older woman prepared a meal for them both. They now enjoyed a more relaxed and much improved relationship.

This situation continued for over 18 months until Kim suddenly came under pressure. For no clear reason she had missed her injection early on in a week when she also suffered a couple of disappointments. First, she failed to get on a vocational course she wanted to do at the local college and, second, her application for a disability living allowance was turned down. When she heard about the latter, the CPN was quite happy to help Kim appeal against this decision but she was now having trouble catching up with her client to give her an injection, let alone help with her finances.

Before long, Kim had missed two injections and her landlord was becoming very concerned about her. He rang the CPN to report that his lodger had started staying out at nights without letting him know beforehand. Things went downhill very quickly from this point and Kim went to a great deal of trouble to avoid seeing the CPN. The landlord got in touch with the nurse again after a week or so because Kim was not only behaving in a bizarre and unpredictable manner, but she also seemed to be depressed; he had the impression she wasn't eating much and she certainly didn't seem to be sleeping.

Shortly after this, Kim took two overdoses in one week. She was sorted out by staff in Casualty and then seen by a psychiatric registrar who sent her home on both occasions. By this time, Kim's mother and the CPN were asking for Kim to be admitted to hospital, with the latter pointing out to doctors and the social work team that her client had made so much progress over 18 months that it should be possible to get over this crisis if they could get her back onto medication before she started abusing drugs again. The nurse had caught up with Kim now but she was refusing adamantly to have an injection or to consider taking any tablets either.

Nothing happened until a week or so later when the landlord telephoned the hospital late one night and said he had just heard that Kim had threatened her mother with a bread-knife earlier that evening and now he had tripped over her sitting out in the garden barefoot in the snow talking to herself. The following afternoon an ASW called at the landlord's house with a psychiatrist and a second doctor – not the GP as he was away on holiday – to assess the young woman. None of them had met Kim before and the CPN had suggested it might be helpful if she came along to the assessment. The offer was not taken up.

The visiting professionals met an intelligent young woman who was lucid and making cynical remarks about this new law against sitting barefoot in the snow. As they got up to leave, the landlord followed them to the door to point out that the incident in the snow was one of a long list of disturbing things which Kim had been up to, including threatening her mother with a knife and being rushed to Casualty twice the previous week after taking an overdose. Much to his frustration, the visitors nodded politely and went away.

Ten days later, the landlord rang the CPN to tell her that he had spent an hour in the middle of the night persuading Kim not to throw herself out of an upstairs window; she seemed suddenly to have so much strength that the landlord had thought they would both fall to the ground before he could manage to shut the window. Anyway, he couldn't take any more; if someone didn't do something, Kim would have to go.

Another mental health assessment was arranged and the CPN made sure that the new psychiatrist and ASW were aware of what had been going on for the past two months and how well Kim had responded to medication in the past. On this occasion, the GP would take part in the assessment. Kim was subdued and polite throughout the professionals' visit and once again there was no evidence of the bizarre behaviour described by the mother, landlord and CPN. However, when Kim firmly dismissed the suggestion that there must be a reason why everyone seemed very worried about her, the GP challenged this, reminding his patient of similar events which had occurred before her previous admissions to hospital. At this point, Kim became agitated and the doctor persevered, questioning her further, enough to persuade himself and his medical colleague to recommend the patient's admission to hospital before they left shortly afterwards.

Nevertheless, there was no Section. It seemed that when the ASW stayed on to consider whether or not to make the application for the young woman's admission to hospital, he had talked with Kim on her own for a while. Kim had continued to show no sign of serious mental illness and had explained that her landlord was trying to get rid of her because he wanted to give his room to a relative who needed lodgings. She had also told the ASW that the CPN had been helpful in the past but she avoided her nowadays because she fussed too much; this rather confirmed the impression the ASW had herself gained of the nurse earlier in the day! As for her mother, Kim pointed out that she had refused to let her daughter return to her home after she first became ill; that was how much she really cared about her. Kim had even been prepared to discuss her overdoses, explaining that these had been a foolish reaction to her learning that the landlord wanted rid of her ...

In short, it seemed, the ASW felt that any bizarre behaviour was probably due to Kim's drug habit and not to mental illness and agreed with the young woman that it was about time that she was allowed to get on with her own life. And that, it seemed, was that. He let the doctors and CPN know his decision and accepted the latter's offer to pass the news on to the mother as she was about to visit her.

Late that night Kim came home shouting abuse at her landlord for telling lies about her. The man felt betrayed by the lack of support he'd received from the system and he'd had enough of what seemed to him to be a completely thankless task. He told Kim he wanted her to leave by lunchtime the next day. In the event, his lodger left in the early hours of the morning, before the landlord had a chance to speak to her mother.

She has not seen her daughter for three years. Twice during the weeks after Kim went missing, the older woman came home to a smashed window and a raided fridge and took some comfort from the fact that Kim had probably come looking for her mother and had cut her losses when she didn't find her at home! She explains that this gives her hope that Kim is still alive and that she'll see her again one day.

COMMENT

This is one of those worrying cases where a sufferer has slipped through the net despite the fact that several agencies and professionals were involved with her during the weeks before this happened. Moreover, throughout this time her mother, her landlord and her CPN were all seeking help for Kim, and pleading for her to be admitted to hospital for treatment. It might well be argued that Kim had sought this help for herself as well by taking two overdoses. There was ample evidence of a pending crisis in a young person who was known to have a serious mental illness.

Before going on to read the LEAP group's analysis of what happened in this case, you might find it worthwhile to pause here and make a note of any factors you can find which seem to have led to Kim being allowed to slip through the net? Do you feel these were due to the system or to individual workers' interpretation of the system?

GROUP'S ANALYSIS OF THE CASE STUDY

When they came to consider this case, group members found it very worrying that the system had failed to protect this young woman from her illness. They felt that this family's tragedy could have been prevented by effective use of the mental health legislation and they were at a loss to understand why this had not been achieved. They set out to try to determine where things went wrong.

First mental health assessment

The group were encouraged to learn that the GP wasted no time when he saw how ill Kim was and that no time was lost by those assessing her in getting her into hospital.

First discharge from hospital

The group were not so impressed with the after-care arrangements made for Kim following her first discharge from hospital. They felt that there were two very clear reasons for suspecting she might prove to be vulnerable; first, her late father's longstanding psychotic illness and, second, her drug habit. Members believed that, ideally, Kim should have been allocated someone to keep an eye on her but, at least, she should have been followed up immediately she started avoiding the GP and psychiatrist. Members felt that at this point she was a disaster waiting to happen; the doctors should have responded to the mother's appeal for help.

'Instead they claimed they couldn't intervene because her daughter wasn't seeking their help and anyway there wasn't an emergency', grumbled a carer. Another carer reminded the group that 'we saw this phenomenon several times in cases we analyzed in *Getting into the System* (the first book in this series), didn't we? With families seeking help because their relative was relapsing only to be told that professionals couldn't intervene because the sufferer wasn't asking them for help!'

The rest of the group were agreed that this sort of response was not acceptable; it suggested a complete ignorance of psychotic behaviour in the very people who work with serious mental illness. As one member who has had several breakdowns put it, 'the last thing I would do if I was relapsing is to seek help from a doctor – surely everyone knows that's the time we can't and don't seek help for ourselves?' Yes, the rest of the group felt this was a reasonable assumption and this led to their wondering whether the reaction of this GP and psychiatrist (and that of other professionals in previous cases they had analyzed) were based on ignorance of this classic feature of a psychotic illness, or was it a 'cop out' by professionals who had learned that the system didn't back them up if they tried to take preventive action? At this point, the group moved on, knowing that this subject would come up for discussion again.

Meanwhile, members had no doubt at all that the doctors could, and should, have intervened at this point, instead of doing nothing. A survivor felt that it was a great pity that mother and daughter were left alone to cope with a potentially dangerous and worsening situation. She thought this was particularly sad as it led to the mother becoming ill herself and this in turn had persuaded her that she couldn't cope with Kim living at home any more. A carer agreed with this, saying, 'That's right, and that didn't help either of them in the long run; the mother shouldn't have been put through this trauma – it was unnecessary'.

Second mental health assessment

The group was encouraged once more by the speedy way in which Kim's second admission was arranged; as before, those carrying out the mental health assessment had no doubts that she should be admitted to hospital, 'and they didn't mess around putting her on a 28-day section again; they made sure there'd be enough time for her to make a good recovery and that's how it should be!' applauded a survivor who owed her own present good health to a similar decision when it mattered.

Treatment and after-care

Members were equally impressed with Kim's stay in hospital, where she was stabilized on a depot injection, and provided with good lodgings and a CPN to keep an eye on her and monitor her medication when she was discharged. Several members described the social worker's contribution to Kim's care by finding the right kind of landlord for her as 'first-class' and no one could fault the planning which went into the young woman's second discharge from hospital.

Someone pointed out that, 'this is one of the advantages of a Section 3 as discharge requires social services and the health authority to provide after-care'. 'Yes', another member agreed, 'and this is one very good reason for making sure that someone who is known to have a serious mental illness is admitted under Section 3!' (1)

The group were agreed that every effort possible had been made to ensure that Kim survived out in the community this time and there was every reason to suppose that she received considerable support from everyone involved with her after-care. So why did things go wrong?

A slippery slope

One or two members wondered why the CPN had been unable to catch up with Kim in time to avoid her being late with having the first injection, let alone missing the next. One carer repeated the concern he had shown with two of the cases in *Getting into the System* where professionals had seen no immediate urgency to intervene when a sufferer missed an injection. He appreciated that the nurse did everything she could later but he stressed, 'I wish she could have concentrated on ensuring that Kim didn't have time to even think about not having her medication!' No one disagreed with this viewpoint; the more cases the LEAP group members have contact with, the more convinced they are that persevering with medication is the first priority in keeping a psychosis at bay and staying well.

A cry for help?

Members were sad to note that a real opportunity for 'the system' to intervene and help Kim was missed; not just once, but twice. They felt that Kim's overdoses were cries for help and that the young woman was clearly depressed, or desperate to find a way out of her crisis; or both. Either way, a carer pointed out, 'alarm bells should have been ringing. Didn't psychiatric staff at Casualty have any information on Kim? Didn't they seek any when she turned up a second time? What an awful waste of a chance to help her!'

'Yes', agreed another member who has personal experience of psychotic breakdown, 'and after that it was too late; Kim wasn't going to accept any help from that point on!' The group found this very sad, particularly as her mother, her landlord and her CPN would all continue to seek this for her 'and would be treated very cavalierly by the system', as another survivor put it.

Third mental health assessment

Members were not at all impressed with this assessment. First, they didn't understand why the professionals involved did not take advantage of the CPN's offer to accompany them to the landlord's home in view of the fact that none of them had met Kim before. As one mother put it, 'Here was a chance for them to ask the right questions and, better still, to be in a position to challenge Kim's answers when she attempted to sidetrack them. Instead, all they could say later was that she had not acted in the way that the three people most involved had reported!' 'But, then, I can't see how they could expect her to, do you?', a carer asked. 'No', agreed a survivor, 'but there always seems to be this tendency for professionals to err on the side of caution and this attitude usually does the sufferer more harm than good'.

There was general agreement that nothing was achieved – nor could be hoped to be achieved – in this seemingly cursory assessment and a carer pointed out that 'the ASW had up to 14 days to complete this assessment and really should have persevered with it' (2).

This last comment touched on an issue which concerned members; they were unhappy about the way a decision could be made not to section without the professionals involved providing any alternative solution. 'As so often seems to happen, things were just left to go on as before until another crisis occurred', a survivor pointed out. Other members agreed and they did not believe this was in the spirit of the law and felt they should look at this further when they had finished this analysis.

Fourth mental health assessment

Members noted that this time at least one person present – the GP – knew Kim and her recent history. 'Because of this, he knew what questions to ask and succeeded in showing that Kim was putting on an act!', a carer observed.

'But the ASW didn't want to know about that, did he?', exclaimed a member who has herself deceived social workers on more than one occasion when she's been psychotic and desperate to avoid detection. 'It's quite scary, really, that some professionals don't appreciate how far we will go to protect ourselves.'

'Yes,' a carer remarked ruefully, 'the ASW seemed more interested in accepting Kim's dismissal of each of the three persons trying to help her – you wouldn't think that a mother, a landlord and a professional could all be wrong, would you?' Another carer said he found this very worrying and, so far as he could see, 'the assessment was not carried out in the spirit of the Mental Health Act or under the professional guidelines contained in the Code of Practice which require the overall medical history to be looked at and others to be consulted properly'.

'That's right, and he apparently ignored the opinion of two doctors and the reports of the three people closest to Kim', a survivor commented. 'How can the system possibly be expected to work when that can happen?'

Rights of the nearest relative

Someone had asked earlier whether or not the mother was the nearest relative and everyone had rightly supposed this must be the case, as she was the sole remaining parent and Kim did not have a partner. This was of particular interest to some members of the group because two doctors had recommended the young woman's admission to hospital by the time the ASW had refused to make the application. This being the case, the nearest relative could make the application instead and the ASW who declined to make the application had a duty to advise the nearest relative of her right to do this and to tell her how to go about using this right (3). 'But apparently the ASW didn't even speak to the mother himself but let the CPN pass on the message that her daughter hadn't been sectioned and that's not good enough, either' a carer pointed out.

Members decided to take a closer look at the rights of the nearest relative later, particularly as at least two members of the group were rather confused at this point.

Finally, members felt very sad that Kim slipped through the net and that her mother has no idea of her whereabouts nor how she is faring. They were particularly concerned about the professional practice of the ASW concerned with this last mental health assessment and felt this was the point at which the system finally failed this vulnerable young woman.

THE WIDER PERSPECTIVE

There were three issues which arose in this analysis, all concerned with crisis intervention, which members felt they would like to explore further.

Reluctance to use the law?

As we noted, the group was exasperated by the failure of the doctors to intervene and 'stop the rot' when Kim started to relapse after her first discharge from hospital. They wondered when they first heard about this whether these professionals (and many others like them) could possibly be ignorant enough about psychosis to be unaware that its victims do not accept they need medical help. They now dismissed this as 'too absurd', as one carer put it. Instead, members felt that the more likely reason for the system turning its back on families at the point when sufferers are clearly relapsing was the phenomenon which cropped up several times when they were working on *Getting into the System*; as one member put it, 'we're back to the situation where many professionals can't accept that a sufferer can be sectioned "in the interests of his own health", aren't we ?'(4)

Other members agreed that this was almost certainly the case and that the doctors shared this misconception. Or they had perhaps found in the past that their professional colleagues would not back them by acknowledging this as a legal ground for sectioning somebody with a serious mental illness who was deteriorating for the want of treatment. 'Yes', added a carer, 'so many professionals still insist that sufferers must be a danger to themselves or others before they're sectionable – I think this is a real liability for sufferers. Don't they realize the risks in delaying things this way?'

'I don't know', sighed a survivor 'but I just wish that professionals who are meant to be helping us stay well would just realize that they are doing us no favours at all by waiting for a crisis each time – why can't they understand that untreated symptoms are bad news and just make things worse for everyone in the end?' (5)

Why, indeed? This summed up the general feeling of the group, with members being well aware that the Department of Health has been stressing throughout the 1990s that the law does allow for a sufferer to be sectioned 'in the interests of his health'.

Leaving a crisis unresolved

When discussing Kim's third mental health assessment, the group had touched on the apparent futility of leaving a crisis like this unresolved. It seemed to them that a mental health assessment has become an 'all or nothing' lottery in which the sufferer either receives care and treatment or nothing at all, leaving the family still in crisis.

'Actually, it's worse than nothing', a carer pointed out, 'because when the professionals walk out on the situation, things are infinitely worse than before they arrived – the sufferer becomes even more uptight and just explodes when they've gone!' This was how it had been for another carer's family too and she said firmly, 'Yes, and this experience lives with you – you think very hard before you seek help another time; in fact, unless you're lucky a mental health assessment becomes just one more obstacle to stumble over'.

The carer who had pointed out earlier that an ASW had up to 14 days to complete a mental health assessment now explained his point further, 'if the social worker had persevered after this first assessment, returning to check up on things – a couple of times, say, over the next few days – then not only would the landlord have felt supported and valued, but the social worker could have gradually obtained a better insight into what was really going on'.

This made sense to the rest of the group, who couldn't see how the existing 'all or nothing' service could be run effectively or economically, let alone in the best interests of families in crisis. Members knew of cases where it had taken three mental health assessments before sufferers received the care and treatment they urgently needed. They felt sure that this was not the way the system was meant to work. It seemed to them that in a situation where family, friends or professionals were seeking admission to hospital for a sufferer, then it was not acceptable for professionals to 'pass through' and just walk away from the situation without offering some sort of on-going help until the crisis was resolved.

'But isn't that because the law sometimes seems to be used as an excuse not to act rather than as a tool for change?' someone asked. Yes, members felt it was. There were provisions in the law, they decided, which were intended to protect sufferers from damaging delays. Instead, mental health assessments tended to be seen as a last resort and, in some cases, just 'one more obstacle to stumble over' as a member had remarked earlier.

It helps to be clearly mad!

It was at this point that someone in the group pointed out the outcome of the first two mental health assessments in this case as compared with the outcome of the third and fourth assessment. Members didn't have much trouble with this apparent anomaly. In the first two instances, they pointed out, Kim was running berserk and, importantly, had become uncontrollable. Those involved in her assessments almost certainly had little choice but to find a way of restraining her quickly; the law provided the means to do this.

'Yes, and sadly this was not the case with the last two assessments', a member observed, 'on these occasions Kim was not running berserk; instead she was deeply troubled, almost certainly suicidal, but also paranoid enough to contain herself when strangers came to assess her'.

'In other words, your chances of getting sectioned depend on your performance on the day', grinned a survivor, 'regardless of all the evidence and whatever sane people around you have to say!' However, in company with the rest of the group, she found this very frustrating.

The nearest relative – the alternative applicant

Several LEAP group members were not too clear about the role of the nearest relative, particularly when it came to sectioning. Others in the group explained to them that the nearest relative is the only person other than an ASW who has the right to make application for a sufferer's admission to hospital. Normally this right would only be exercised by the nearest relative, given that the required medical back-up was available, if an ASW had declined to make the application, as was the case after Kim's fourth assessment.

During the discussion which followed, two parents in the group who had just taken an active part in explaining this aspect of the law each told us how they had not had this information when they needed it: 'I didn't even know there was such an animal as a nearest relative when my son got ill,' one exclaimed, 'let alone that that was me (6) and that I could have got him into hospital without all the aggro and misery which followed'. Both these carers were confident that it would have made a considerable difference to the outcome of their own relative's crisis if they had known their rights at that time. Sadly, they are not alone in this; the Northwick Park Study of First Episodes of Schizophrenia (7) revealed that other families have had similar experiences.

When members of the group asked these two carers if they would take advantage of this right if they found themselves in the same situation again, both said 'yes' quite emphatically, after only the slightest pause. Nevertheless, they went on to explain they would much prefer an ASW to make the application for their relative to be sectioned. This, of course, is how the system should work; it's widely appreciated that this is an awesome responsibility to foist on someone close to the sufferer and one that can sometimes spoil the future relationship of the two people concerned. Nevertheless, members agreed that this right provides a vital safety net when all else fails and one that could have served Kim and her mother well.

'But', someone asked, 'how can the system work properly if "new" families – and lots of not so new families, come to that – don't know about the law and about nearest relatives, let alone their rights?' 'Well, quite', responded one of the carers who had been there, 'when it matters, you can be totally dependent upon the ASW to tell you your rights. That's OK if the ASW is not one of those who is biased against the use of the law to detain someone in hospital – and they do exist, more's the pity!'

After some discussion on this rather surprising and vexing state of affairs, group members concluded that it should not be too difficult to ensure that a reluctant ASW could be persuaded to adhere to the law and to good professional practice. They were baffled that the system in general and social services departments in particular haven't addressed this matter. 'After all', a carer concluded, 'they, or the social worker, could presumably be sued for negligence if the rights of the nearest relative had been abused at the sufferer's expense?' Yes, other members thought that must surely be the case.

SUMMING UP

While members of the LEAP group were most impressed with the treatment and support which Kim received once her real vulnerability was recognized, they were unhappy about several aspects of the way the system responded both times she relapsed.

Issues which concerned them were (a) missed opportunities to use the law to help Kim during her first relapse, (b) mental health assessments which seem to provide 'all or nothing' for a family in crisis, and (c) a situation where nearest relatives may not be aware of rights which might resolve the sufferer's psychotic crisis.

INFORMATION

The following pieces of information are relevant to points brought up during the group's analysis and discussion which have been highlighted in the text.

(1) The appropriate use of Section 3

See Chapter 3 in the present book for a discussion on a 'least restrictive' practice which some ASWs and other professionals seem to interpret as imposing the least restraint possible on a sufferer if compulsory admission cannot be avoided. This discussion argues that a 'least restrictive' practice can involve poor professional practice and be prejudicial to the sufferer's future welfare.

(2) Extra time to determine whether or not to section

As a member of the LEAP group has stated here, the Mental Health Act 1983 allows for ASWs taking some considerable time to come to a decision about whether or not to section someone. The Code of Practice points out in paragraph 2.26: 'Most compulsory admissions require prompt action to be taken but it should be remembered that the ASW has up to 14 days from the date of first seeing the patient to make an application for admission for assessment or treatment'.

(3) Nearest relative as alternative applicant

See paragraph 2.27 on page 12 of the Code of Practice, Mental Health Act 1983.

(4) A neglected ground for sectioning

One of the grounds for compulsory admission to hospital under the Mental Health Act 1983 is in the interests of the patient's health.

The last paragraph of the foreword to the Code of Practice states:

> It has been widely reported that the criteria for admission to hospital under the Act have not been correctly understood by all professionals. In particular, there is said to have been a misconception that patients may only be admitted under the Act if there is a risk to their own or other people's safety. In fact, the Act provides for admission in the interests of the patient's health, or of his or her safety, or for the protection of other people. This is clearly spelt out in the new paragraph 2.6 of the Code (pp. iii and 4 of the Code of Practice)

(5) The dangers in long delays in obtaining appropriate treatment

(a) Richard Jed Wyatt has concluded, in his comprehensive overview of the use of neuroleptic medication and the natural course of schizophrenia that 'some patients are left with a damaging residual if a psychosis is allowed to proceed unmitigated. While psychosis is undoubtedly demoralizing and stigmatizing, it may also be biologically toxic'. (Wyatt,R J 'Neuroleptics and the natural course of schizophrenia.' *Schizophrenia Bulletin, 17,* 2, 1991)

(b) In a large extended study of first episodes of schizophrenia, Dr Tim Crow and his colleagues found the delay between onset of symptoms and admission to hospital to be a significant factor in predicting poor outcome in a schizophrenic illness. The most important determinant of relapse was duration of illness prior to starting neuroleptic medication (Crow, T. J. *et al.* (1986) The Northwick Park Study of First Episodes of Schizophrenia, Part II: A randomized controlled trial of prophylactic neuroleptic treatment. *British Journal of Psychiatry 148,* 120–7)

(6) Identifying the nearest relative

The Mental Health Act 1983 defines the nearest relative with the following list, in order of priority:

- husband or wife
- son or daughter
- father or mother

- brother or sister
- grandparent
- grandchild
- uncle or aunt
- nephew or niece

Where two relatives have equal priority, then the elder will be the choice, with half-blood relationships taking second place. Where the patient normally resides with a relative, then that one will be the nearest relative. If the patient has lived with a non-relative as husband or wife for at least six months prior to admission to hospital then that person is considered to be the nearest relative (unless one has now deserted the other). If the patient has lived with a non-relative, but not as husband or wife, for five years, then the person is considered to be a relative, but not necessarily the nearest relative.

(7) Nearest relatives unaware of their rights

E. C. Johnstone and her colleagues reported in The Northwick Park Study of First Episodes of Schizophrenia, Part I, (1986) *British Journal of Psychiatry 148*, 115–120, various factors which hindered families in their efforts to obtain help for their relative and commented that 'several difficult situations could have been avoided had the relatives known that they themselves could make application for the patient's admission under the Mental Health Act.'

As we have noted, two members of the LEAP group had found themselves similarly disadvantaged.

EXERCISE

Imagine you have been commissioned by the Department of Health to consider ways of ensuring that mental health assessments always focus on resolving the reported crisis and that they lead to the provision of support for the sufferer and family until that is achieved. You have also been told that no change in the law or additional funding is envisaged.

Detail your recommendations.

CHAPTER 3

A 'least restrictive' practice?

Sometimes social workers and other professionals working with the mental health legislation have been persuaded to believe that the best way to protect the rights of those who do need to be sectioned is to make sure their detention covers the shortest possible time. Such action can have a profound effect on a sufferer's chances of becoming well again. Sharon's story demonstrates this.

CASE STUDY

A usually cheerful, contented girl, Sharon became seriously depressed when she was 15 years old and the family's GP helped her through this by prescribing anti-depressants which she took for six months or so. By the time she came off the tablets, Sharon was her old self and had no trouble at all catching up with her studies. An exceptionally bright girl, she went on to obtain the sort of 'A' level results that ensured she would be able to fulfil her plans to study to become a vet.

Sharon went off to university 200 miles from home and halfway through her first term at college, she was admitted to hospital suffering with a manic episode. It seemed that she had suddenly become the life and soul of her college almost overnight and rushed around on a high organizing everyone around her for the best part of a week without pausing for rest, let alone sleep. The new friends she had made at college were at first surprised, then they were swept along by her creative enthusiasm and, finally, they became seriously worried. At that point, a tutor whom they felt able to approach, suggested Sharon walk back with her to the main buildings at the end of a lecture and then insisted in just popping into see one of the GPs who 'serviced' the university, having sought his co-operation earlier. After a social chat, as Sharon seemed to see it (during which the young woman never stopped talking) the doctor attempted to explain that he thought she should go into hospital. She appeared to be agreeable and co-operative about this. Perhaps predictably, this did not last when she finally realized later that the doctor wanted her to stay there. At this point, he asked for a mental health assessment to be arranged and, with someone keeping a careful eye on her for the rest of the day, Sharon was eventually admitted to the hospital on Section 2, allowing for her to be detained up to 28 days for assessment followed by treatment if appropriate.

Once she was in hospital, the supervising psychiatrist went about obtaining Sharon's medical history and learned that her GP at home had treated her for a serious depression a few years earlier. He decided to prescribe lithium as her mood was still very elevated two weeks after her admission and, a month or so later, Sharon was well enough to be discharged and was transferred to the care of a psychiatrist in her home town. The new psychiatrist told Sharon and her widowed mother that although this might well be a manic depressive illness (MD), the hospital team who had been treating her felt that her prognosis was excellent. After the Christmas holidays, Sharon seemed fit and was anxious to return to college where she soon caught up on the work she had missed. Six months later, at the end of her first college year, her psychiatrist agreed with her request that she could now be weaned off her lithium treatment.

During the following term, no one at college noted that anything was amiss; Sharon seemed to be coping well enough but, once home again for the Christmas break, she was soon causing her family concern. They noted that she was sleeping very little, if at all, and her mood was high much of the time. It seemed to her mother and two brothers that she never stopped talking, mainly about unlikely plans for the immediate future which made no sense at all to them. When they tried to discuss their concern with her, Sharon became quite hostile, telling them that they were fussing too much and acting as if she hadn't enough sense to look after herself.

Things went from bad to worse and the holiday was a disaster with Sharon having to be admitted to hospital on Boxing Day. By that time her behaviour was so bizarre and uninhibited that professionals carrying out the mental health assessment had no doubt that she needed to be in hospital. The ASW explained to Sharon's mother that it seemed a shame to have to admit her under section but she could see no alternative so she would apply for a 28-day order as she and her colleagues would not want to restrain her for a longer period.

In hospital, Sharon was hallucinating and severely deluded but her symptoms responded quickly to the anti-psychotic drugs she was prescribed. However, her mood remained high as before and two weeks later she was put back on lithium. Just as her psychiatrist realized that his patient was making real progress at last, Sharon announced to the ward staff that as her 28-day section had expired a few days earlier she was now going home. The psychiatrist, who had not been involved in Sharon's mental health assessment, told her that this would be premature and he could not agree to what she was suggesting. When the young woman said that didn't matter as she would discharge herself, he felt unable to do anything; it seemed he did not believe she was sectionable at this time. He arranged for a CPN to follow up his patient as quickly as possible.

On her return home, Sharon initially seemed quite well but it soon became clear that this was not the case. When her new CPN made reference to her recent illness, Sharon flared up angrily, denying having been ill; 'my family set me up', she told the nurse, 'because they didn't want me around for Christmas'. Not long afterwards, the CPN reported to the psychiatrist that Sharon had no insight at all into her illness and was already threatening to come off her medication. Later, she supported the family in their efforts to persuade Sharon to keep taking her lithium when she returned to college. Her mother reminded her how important her studies were if she was to achieve her long ambition to become a vet and her daughter seemed to hear this. It seemed that everyone could only hope for the best.

Sharon returned to college but she was home again a month later. She said that her studying had become a bore. She knew what was the matter; she was fed up at just playing at being an adult. It was time she grew up and found herself a proper job, she'd decided. She would go and earn a living, however modest; with her beloved animals of course. Once again she seemed unable to stop talking and it was soon clear that Sharon was not sleeping and was feeling very hostile about the family once more.

After ringing the college and learning that her daughter had not attended more than a couple of lectures since her return, her mother then tried to contact the CPN but was told she was off sick. Similarly, when she phoned Sharon's psychiatrist, she had to content herself with leaving a message for him with his secretary. Could he please help? Sharon was home from college, off her medication and showing all the signs of becoming manic. He did not return her call, nor was there any other sort of response to her further calls for help from him and the CPN team.

A week later, Sharon had to be compulsorily admitted to hospital. Neither the psychiatrist nor the ASW knew her but there was no doubt in their minds that she was urgently in need of care and treatment. When the mother was told once more that Sharon would be admitted on a Section 2, she queried this, explaining to the ASW that, after her daughter's last sectioning, she had learned that Section 2 was meant to be mainly for assessment purposes whereas Section 3 allowed for treatment and up to six months in hospital for individuals already known to have a serious mental illness. As the nearest relative, she was now asking him to admit her daughter on a Section 3 because Sharon had discharged herself too soon last time although the psychiatrist had wanted to keep her in hospital. The ASW replied that if that was the case, he should have done so. The mother didn't know what to say at this point as she had been told at the hospital that the doctor had no powers to do this; she just didn't know who to believe. Despairingly, she walked away, too confused to continue to fight her case.

Sharon was again admitted on a Section 2. Her mother and her two sons talked with hospital staff about their attempts to have her admitted on a longer section; nurses on the ward who knew Sharon agreed this might have been more satisfactory and promised to talk with her psychiatrist about this. The family heard no more. Both brothers tried telephoning the doctor during the next two weeks, again to no avail. Two days after her section expired, Sharon discharged herself and once more before the psychiatrist felt she was well enough to leave hospital. He tried to persuade her to listen to reason but she became angry and told him 'you just want to put me away, don't you?'.

When she came home, it quickly became clear that the young woman had no more insight into her illness than the last time she had left hospital and, accordingly, blamed her mother for putting her away again. The CPN was still off sick and Sharon's mother tried in vain to contact the psychiatrist, phoning several times and leaving messages when she did so. Finally, she wrote him a long and passionate letter explaining what Sharon's illness was doing to the whole family and seeking his help. Again, she received no reply.

Not long afterwards, Sharon moved out of the family home, saying her mother and brothers were the cause of all her problems. She now only gets in touch with them when she is in trouble of some sort. She has, for instance, asked for help several times in the three years since she left home when she has needed to find new digs immediately because other tenants have complained about the disturbances she causes. She continues to have no insight whatever into the way she behaves, let alone the cause for this. She rarely takes her medication for more than a few days after returning from her now frequent admissions to hospital.

Sharon is restless, bored and lonely. She bitterly resents failing in everything she tries to do. She now bears little resemblance to the able girl who set out to achieve a lifelong ambition to be a vet. Her mother is devastated about what has happened to her daughter and believes that things could have been different. She is hurt and bewildered that mental health professionals took so little notice of the family's efforts to protect Sharon from the more obvious risks incurred by her illness; her sons are vocal and angry about this but have no more idea than their mother how to make Sharon understand that she still matters to them.

COMMENT

This is one of those unhappy cases where a serious mental illness has been allowed to destroy a family's natural coping mechanisms. Despite their determined efforts, Sharon is now bitterly unhappy and alienated from her mother and brothers, believing they are responsible for all her problems.

It is arguable that this family have every right to feel they have been let down as well as feeling bereaved of a daughter and sister. Perhaps you would like to pause for a moment and consider how you might feel about this case if you were Sharon's mother or one of her brothers? How do you think that the service your family received could have been improved? Do you feel that Sharon's wellbeing was put at risk by any aspects of this service?

GROUP'S ANALYSIS OF CASE STUDY

Members were particularly frustrated by this unhappy case because the mother and brothers were treated as if they didn't exist although they were the ones who had so much to lose if no one heeded their pleas for help. Members had only come across one other case – Barry, featured in Chapter 4 of *Getting into the System* (the first book in this series) where the family had been treated so badly by professionals meant to be looking after the best interests of their relative.

First signs of illness

It seemed to the group that the GP's response to Sharon's depression at 15 years was effective as she clearly became well enough to get on with her studies and qualify for training to be a vet. Whether or not she was strong enough by that time to go away from home was another matter. It is easy to be wise after the event, but there was a strong feeling that the signs were there that Sharon might be vulnerable.

First manic episode

It seemed to members that Sharon came through this first manic episode as well as could be expected with fellow students and staff making a concerted effort to arrange help for her, rather than ignore the problem until there was a real crisis as sometimes happens when sufferers are away from home. She then responded quickly to treatment but it seemed clear by then that her earlier depression had heralded a mood disorder and that she was probably suffering with MD.

The general feeling in the group at that point was that the outlook seemed to be fairly positive nevertheless. However, a carer wanted to know why doctors had assumed that Sharon's prognosis was excellent? 'Even though she responded quickly to medication, her mood was high enough to necessitate her being put on lithium and she'd already suffered with depression earlier, hadn't she?', she asked. Yes, others in the group also wondered about this over-confident prognosis and felt this may have served to convince Sharon she had nothing to worry about. Just how much were she and the family told about MD at this time, they wondered?

Several members also wanted to know why Sharon wasn't encouraged to stay on her lithium now she was doing so well on this?

As one mother put it, 'she had already demonstrated that being at college could make her vulnerable and she still had a long way to go at that stage; this was all new to her and a time of change!' Another carer agreed with 'I know I'm always saying this, but I do wish doctors would see it is as good news when sufferers do well on medication rather than confirmation that they should come off it!'

Second manic episode and mental health assessment

It seemed to the group that the mental health assessment arranged for Sharon when she had her second manic episode was probably as painless as one could hope for considering that the crisis broke in the middle of a Christmas holiday. However, it was clearly not through an oversight that she was admitted on a Section 2 rather than a Section 3. The ASW had told the mother they didn't want to 'restrain' her daughter for more than 28 days. Group members were well aware that everything pointed to Sharon being admitted on a Section 3 which allows an extended period for treatment of a sufferer already diagnosed and known to the local mental health team (1). LEAP group was alerted to this issue because of the tragic results members have seen in sufferers known to them who haven't had time to properly recover from a relapse on a 28-day section. This, indeed, is what now happened to Sharon.

'I don't understand this,' a carer remarked, 'the ASW talked of not wishing to restrain Sharon for more than 28 days. Such a preconceived idea of how long one should be admitted to hospital seems odd. Whether a section allows for up to 28 days or up to 6 months is not the issue – sections can be discharged by the psychiatrist supervising the case at any time or, for that matter, renewed'.

'Yes,' laughed a second carer, 'some of us know one sufferer who was admitted under a Section 3 and his psychiatrist discharged the section the next day because he agreed to stay in hospital. He was discharged three weeks later because of a shortage of beds – I can see that might make those doing an assessment on this doctor's patients think twice another time!'

Despite one or two similar bizarre examples, members felt it a shame that the ASW in this assessment preferred to restrain Sharon for as short a time as possible rather than use the longer section which was designed to allow ample time for the treatment she might need. Nevertheless, and rather sadly, there was no doubt in members' minds that the social worker was genuinely trying to look after Sharon's interests and to protect her from any avoidable distress, however misguided they knew her decision to be.

Second manic episode: treatment and after-care

The group noted that although Sharon's bizarre symptoms responded well to anti-psychotic drugs, her local psychiatrist decided, like the previous one, that she needed to be stabilized on lithium. It seemed that he felt she was beginning to make real progress just at the time that her section expired. It was not clear whether or not he had been concerned, or even conscious, about the length of this until Sharon decided she needn't stay on once it expired. However, it was clear that he felt he could do nothing to keep her in hospital longer.

They also noted that when the doctor's thinking on this was challenged by the ASW, Sharon's mother became confused and unsure, not knowing who to believe. Several members of LEAP group were also unsure on this point, having assumed the doctor's hands were indeed tied at this stage. Others who are more conversant with the law felt differently and agreed with the carer who declared, 'he could have arranged to have the section converted to a Section 3 at that point; surely he could have demonstrated that his patient wasn't willing to remain in the hospital and accept the further treatment he knew she needed ?'(2)

Either way, although he arranged for a CPN to call, members had no doubt at all that it was a tragic omission on this doctor's part to avoid discussing the dilemma in depth with the family and everyone was sure he should have explained to the mother that Sharon was still very vulnerable. Members were also sure that he should have also provided a lifeline for the mother so that she could have got in touch with a mental health worker when things started going wrong instead of having no choice but to run around leaving unanswered messages for him.

Several members felt the psychiatrist could also have put pressure on Sharon not to go back to college at this point, particularly if he had liaised with the family and, perhaps through them, with the college as well. As it was, the young woman's career ambitions came to a sad end at the point when she went back to college while she was still not well.

As a survivor pointed out, 'Sharon wasn't ready to return to college and it would have been helpful if someone at the college had advised the family that things were not right when it was realized that she wasn't attending her lectures'. 'After all', she added, 'they already knew about Sharon's vulnerability, didn't they?' 'Yes, this family needed all the help they could get', a carer agreed.

Third manic episode and mental health assessment

Members had no doubts at all that this time Sharon should certainly have been admitted on Section 3 for treatment and that Section 2 was not appropriate; the sufferer's recent history made this unarguable in their opinion.

They observed that, as it turned out, Sharon's psychiatrist was again not involved in her assessment – they wondered if he would have successfully challenged another Section 2 for his patient? As it was (and because the doctor had not liaised with the family when Sharon discharged herself) the mother found herself defenceless in her efforts to challenge the system on her own. The group was most impressed by the homework she'd done since the first mental health assessment and was shocked by the reception she got from this ASW. They thought it very sad indeed that the social worker didn't listen to her and properly consider what she was saying. A carer felt angry about this, complaining that 'not only was the ASW involved in poor practice, he was doing Sharon an injustice by not using a Section 3 when she hadn't really recovered from her last breakdown'. 'Yes,' a survivor agreed, 'and he showed no recognition at all of the mother's situation and her desperate struggle to protect her daughter. I find this chilling, I do really!'.

Third manic episode: treatment and after-care

At this point, group members pointed out that the psychiatrist knew his patient had not had a reasonable chance to recover from her recent breakdown and that this was almost certainly because she had discharged herself prematurely. He would have had every justification for immediately arranging for her Section 2 to be converted to a Section 3 on the grounds that the shorter section would not allow enough time for her treatment (3). Why didn't he do this, they wanted to know?

'Perhaps he didn't know his law?', a survivor suggested, 'that might explain his cavalier treatment of the family if he didn't know what he was doing, generally?'

Members knew GPs and psychiatrists who, although expected to work with the law, didn't seem to know much about it. A carer pointed out 'I don't think they have any real training in using the law, do they?' Someone else agreed, 'I think that's right and I get the impression some of them just leave it to the ASW, don't you?' However, another member felt it would be strange if advice and relevant information were not readily available within the hospital and this did seem to be a valid comment. A survivor asked, 'could the doctor have believed he wouldn't be able to persuade an ASW that this was necessary?'

'Well, that didn't have to be a problem, really, because he could then have gone ahead with converting the section with the nearest relative – the mother had made it very clear that she would fight for her daughter's interests', a carer replied.

'We-e-ell', another member mused, 'even if this doctor knew his law, he certainly didn't have any contact whatever with the mother, did he? He'd been busy avoiding her by all counts – could have been awkward in the circumstances!' Yes, members were left with the feeling that the psychiatrist might have felt it was easier to let sleeping dogs lie and this didn't make them feel any more charitable about his treatment of this family.

Members felt sad and frustrated by this case: 'there were only losers here, weren't there?' a carer summed it up, 'a distressed and broken family, a lonely, unfulfilled young woman and a vulnerable sufferer becoming more and more of a burden upon the system'.

THE WIDER PERSPECTIVE

There were two issues which particularly concerned the group when they were working on their analysis of this case study and they decided to look at these more closely now.

The family: a neglected resource

We noted earlier in this chapter that the LEAP group had worked on a case in *Getting into the System* in which a sufferer's family had been treated most of the time as if they didn't exist. They felt that the treatment of Sharon's mother by the psychiatrist and the last ASW was equally reprehensible and even callous.

When the group had analysed the previous case they had considered what they would have wanted from professionals if they had been the sufferer's parents. One member had opted for (a) involvement from the start in a proper care plan; (b) pro-active support and to be given the right information (c) to be treated with some dignity, and, (d) to be recognized as the major provider of community care for the sufferer. As he pointed out now, 'Sharon clearly had no care plan, perhaps because she discharged herself from hospital, but we keep hearing of cases like this and this is very worrying'. It wasn't clear, he felt, whether or not information – about the illness, the role of medication and other important issues – was given to Sharon and her family but he thought that the over-optimistic prognosis might well have precluded the need for such explanations. However, it was very clear that no support was given to the family 'and this mother was certainly not treated with respect', he added. 'The word *humiliation* springs to mind and there was no acknowledgment that she was a single parent struggling to keep her family together, as well as being the nearest relative with her daughter's needs clearly paramount in her mind'.

This was how it seemed to others too and members were quite angry about this mother's treatment. A survivor commented, 'family members often seem to be victims of the mental health services, and this makes no sense at all to me'. A carer stared at her thoughtfully for a moment and then said slowly 'you have just summed up how I feel when my relative has a relapse: I immediately become a *victim!* There is no other time when I'm totally dependent on others, vulnerable, utterly powerless, and sometimes even abused – verbally, that is – in a way that would be unthinkable in my ordinary day-to-day life!'

She went quiet for a moment and then added, almost in tears, 'No, I'm not talking about being abused by my relative – that too sometimes, I suppose, when he's paranoid. No, I mean spoken to by professionals as if I'm the lowest of the low: first, when I try to get help before things get too bad and later, when they eventually respond and feel they can blame me for the battlefield they find'. She finished lamely with 'yes, a victim, that's how I feel ...'.

Three other carers were nodding throughout and one commented, 'Yes, I said to my husband (he's the nearest relative) last time we had a crisis , "no one else ever speaks to you that way, do they?" Really, you wouldn't believe what we have to take from some of them when our son's ill. What right do they have to be like this?'

'Yes', a survivor joined in, 'that's how it used to be for my mother – it's as though being the parent of a sufferer makes one fair game for some professionals – to be judged, criticized and yes, abused! I wonder why?'

A carer volunteered at this point that a psychotic crisis seemed to bring out the worst in everyone at the point when a decision has to be made, 'excepting the sufferer who's usually busy proving he's the only one who's OK' she laughed. 'Perhaps that's why the family theories of schizophrenia (4) were popular; it might be comforting to be able to take it out on someone, particularly if you feel helpless to do anything about all the horror. Better the family than the sufferer, I guess!'

On a more serious note, members brought this contentious and, for some, acutely painful subject to a close, agreeing that they wished they could find a way to 'change the world' and persuade more professionals to work in partnership with families. They felt that what happened to Sharon illustrated this important point very well and that if professionals had communicated and liaised with her mother and brothers, then her story might have ended quite differently.

Mental health assessments: a 'least restrictive' practice?

One mother in the group felt very strongly about Sharon being given less time than she needed to become well again after her second and third breakdowns. As some of the group were already aware, her own family had had experience of this restrictive practice:

'This has been the same with my son, twice now!', she exclaimed. 'The first time it happened, by the time the system caught up with him, he was so ill it took months and months to get him back to how he was before. The trouble was they'd only put him on a 28-day section and he walked out when this finished just as he was beginning to make some progress. A nurse persuaded him to go back but a few weeks later they said they needed his bed. Then, of course, he needed to go into hospital again quite soon and it all happened again. This time I queried the Section 2 – like Sharon's mother – and the ASW said there was no problem; it would be converted on the ward if I was right. It wasn't. Instead, five weeks later we were asked to have my son home one night and then they told us next morning they'd discharged him as they needed the bed.'

When they discussed this member's experience, a survivor asked suddenly, 'Do ASWs get brownie points for taking a "least restrictive" approach or something?'

'I don't really think it can be quite that simple', grinned a carer, 'but, you've got something there because ASWs like this do seem to be passing the buck, don't they? Maybe they don't like the responsibilities which go with the power they have?'

'Yes', a mother joined in, 'I do believe some of them like keeping their hands clean, like its only doctors and families who want to put sufferers away?'

'Yes, but there's another side to this. Those of us who have been there know just how dreadful it is to be sectioned. I'm not at all sure I could cope with being told I could be detained for six months. I'm sure some ASWs must literally smell our fear and hate what they're doing!'

'Yes,' a second survivor agreed, 'I'm sure some ASWs sense our desperation and feel they must do something to protect us in any way they can. This might explain why some ASWs seem to be so hostile to carers too; perhaps they only meet them when they're trying to put someone away!', she added with a smile.

'Well, put like that I could almost see their point', a carer responded in kind, 'but I'm not sure that I agree that it's just the soft ones who tend to refuse to use a Section 3, or to section at all for that matter. We know some very caring ASWs who interpret the law in the same way sort of way that this group does. They don't see a need to protect sufferers from the law; they use it to protect them instead!'

'You're right about it not being the soft ones who avoid sectioning!' another survivor broke in, 'The last time I was ill, I was interviewed by an ASW for well over an hour. Everyone was asking him to section me and he refused to, leaving the responsibility for protecting me to everyone else, but he made me feel as if I'd crawled out from under a bush. He showed me no respect whatever and he did me no favours. I still shudder when I think about him'.

'Yes, and he was engaged in buck-passing from what you say. Now, I guess we've come back to those professionals who are so preoccupied with civil rights that they forget that the most important human right is to be treated with respect and to be treated as if you matter!' ; a previous speaker who 'has been there', spoke with real feeling.

This, it seemed, was the point at which everyone was in agreement; the role of professionals was to see sufferers successfully through a crisis and to do this with compassion and respect for them and their families. Or, to put it another way, to make sure there were no victims?

SUMMING UP

As we have noted, the LEAP group felt that this was a poorly handled case where professionals ignored what was happening to this family and, in doing so, failed to serve the best interests of a young woman with a serious mental illness. Members were particularly concerned that some ASWs seem to be preoccupied with minimizing their use of the law rather than seeing it as a tool which, if used properly, can protect a sufferer from unnecessary damage.

INFORMATION

The following pieces of information are relevant to points brought up during the group's analysis and discussion which have been highlighted in the text:

(1) The use of Section 2 and Section 3

(a) The Mental Health Act 1983 refers to an application for a Section 2 as 'an application for admission for assessment' and to Section 3 as 'an application for admission for treatment' (see pp. 2 and 3).

(b) Paragraphs 5.2 and 5.3 of the *Code of Practice* detail the pointers for selecting a Section 2 or a Section 3 and it is the experience of the LEAP group that the practice of some ASWs in no way reflects the guidance given on this particular aspect of a mental health assessment (see pp. 21–22)

(2) Converting to a Section 3 when a Section 2 is nearly expired

The *Code of Practice* details indicators for using Section 3 under the heading *Section 3 pointers*. Paragraph 5.3 b gives one example:

> where a patient already admitted under section 2 and who is assessed as needing further medical treatment for mental disorder under the Act at the conclusion of his detention under Section 2 is unwilling to remain in hospital informally and to consent to the medical treatment (see p. 22)

(3) Converting to a Section 3 when a Section 2 will not be appropriate or adequate

The *Code of Practice* details indicators for using Section 3 under the heading Section 3 pointers. Paragraph 5.3c gives one example:

> where a patient is detained under section 2 and assessment points to a need for treatment under the Act for a period beyond the 28 day detention under section 2. In such circumstances an application for detention under section 3 should be made at the earliest opportunity and should not be delayed until the end of section 2 detention ... (see p.22)

(4) Family Theories

This LEAP group member was referring to the popular theories which abounded in the 1960s and 1970s and profoundly influenced the received wisdom on one of the two most common psychotic illnesses for at least two decades. Blaming families for their relative's schizophrenia, these theories added significantly to the anguish of carers while detracting attention from more meaningful avenues of research.

Poorly researched and long since discredited, these theories live on in the minds of some of those who influence contemporary thinking. For a full discussion, see *The Reality of Schizophrenia,* Faber and Faber, 1991 (pp.79–81) by the present author.

EXERCISE

In this chapter we have looked at what can happen when professionals believe in using a 'least restrictive practice' approach. Such practice can prejudice the opportunities for sufferers to benefit from those parts of the Mental Health Act which allow for sufferers to be protected from potentially damaging effects of their illness; in particular from unnecessary delays in getting into hospital (i.e., the patient can be admitted in the interests of his health) and from too little time in hospital for treatment to be effective (i.e., for the patient who has a recognized mental illness to be admitted for treatment under a six-month Section 3).

Please imagine you have been asked by the Department of Health to consider a two-part question on their behalf; (a) what it is that persuades some, perhaps many, professionals to avoid using these two aspects of the law ? (b) how does this avoidance of these two aspects of the law actually benefit sufferers and those closest to them?

CHAPTER 4

The role of medication in acute psychosis

Many of those who suffer with an acute psychotic illness can become very well and stay that way so long as they continue to take the medication which protects them from their illness. Without this, their future and their quality of life become entirely dependent upon others being prepared to intervene and take responsibility for their welfare. Cyril's case illustrates just how precarious this can be.

CASE STUDY

A mild, good-natured man, Cyril had several relapses after a first episode of schizophrenia in his late thirties. The last one occurred when he was 62 years old and resulted in an earlier retirement than he would have liked from his long-time clerical job in the local housing department. Two years later, his mother died following a short illness. Not long after this, Cyril moved half a mile or so from the family council house into a one-bedroom flat in a block occupied by people of his own age and older. He was happy with this move and started to take an interest in making the flat into a real home for himself.

Cyril's mother had always worried about what would happen to her only son once he had no one to fend for him when his illness threatened. She had talked about this with June, the CPN who called once a fortnight to give Cyril an injection and the nurse kept a careful eye on Cyril after the older woman's death. Although he couldn't find much to do with his time when he first retired, Cyril gradually settled into a routine after he moved into his new flat. Always an avid reader, he went to the library most weekdays to browse through newspapers and, increasingly, to dip into cookery books which provided simple, no-nonsense recipes. He was enjoying cooking – something there had been no need to do when his mother was alive – and was also taking an interest in DIY ideas too. Before long, Cyril enrolled at a beginners class in woodwork and every so often June would be proudly shown his latest creation for his new home; starting with a shelf for his books and later a pair of bookends.

She was delighted with his progress but she did feel a little concerned about how her favourite client would react when he learned that she would soon be going away for nine months for some extra training in community work.

As it turned out, it seemed she need not have worried; Cyril reacted quite calmly when she told him the news and that she would soon be introducing him to the nurse who would look after her clients while she was away. He smilingly wished her every success on her course. June was glad he now seemed so strong and self-sufficient; so different to the first months after he lost his mother. Things seemed to be all right with Cyril when his new nurse called several times to give him his injection although she was not at all sure he was getting out and about in quite the same way that he did when June was visiting him. However one morning, six weeks or so after June had gone on her course, Cyril answered the door to find two young women, both strangers, on the doorstep and one of them smilingly told him she had come to give him his injection as his nurse was on holiday. Maybe he was embarrassed – more likely he was offended – but something snapped; Cyril angrily sent them both away.

When the usual nurse returned two weeks later, it was now a month since he had had an injection and Cyril told her there was no point in continuing with the injections; he was well, wasn't he? When the nurse protested that it was important not to miss injections, Cyril retorted angrily that he had already missed the last one and no one had worried about that, had they? He was adamant and the nurse was surprised at the change in Cyril since she saw him last; he didn't seem much like the mild and agreeable man she had been getting to know during the past weeks.

Cyril refused to discuss the matter with the CPN or her colleagues, nor would he attend the out-patient appointment that was hurriedly arranged for him. Several months went by and one morning the housing officer responsible for the block of flats where Cyril lived contacted the CPN team; Cyril had paid no rent for 13 weeks and wouldn't discuss this with him. In fact, he had ordered him off his doorstep the last time he called and he suspected that the man was not at all well. The housing officer was concerned as the Council were talking about eviction.

The CPN team got in touch with Cyril's GP. June had introduced him to the doctor when he moved to the new flat and he had gone along to the surgery three or four times during the next twelve months but the doctor had not seen him for some time. He now made a home visit but Cyril would not let him into the flat. When he persisted with his attempt to talk with him, Cyril became verbally abusive and then slammed the door in his visitor's face.

The GP asked Social Services to arrange for his patient to have a mental health assessment, explaining Cyril's history to them. He told them he felt Cyril was looking thin and haggard, probably not feeding himself properly, as well as being hostile and aggressive. According to his notes, he became like this only when he was psychotic and this happened when he stopped taking medication, as now.

When Cyril answered the door a couple of days after the GP had called, he recognized the psychiatrist who had treated him the last time he had been in hospital and quickly told him and the social worker with him that he was not going to go into hospital again. His visitors noted that the flat was clean and tidy. Indeed, so was Cyril, although he was wearing an old mac over his indoor clothes and heavy boots; however the flat was certainly very cold and bare. The psychiatrist also noted that Cyril had aged very rapidly in the past four years but then he knew that during that time his patient's mother had died and he also had to cope with a move from his old home. The psychiatrist remembered that Cyril had been upset by having to give up his work as well; all things considered it was not surprising that he was looking worn.

The ASW spent some time alone with Cyril and later explained to his medical colleague that he couldn't find anything wrong with his reasoning. Cyril was angry because he felt everyone was interfering and intruding on his privacy. The social worker could identify with the older man's feelings and he certainly seemed to be looking after himself and the flat. Cyril had reiterated that he was not prepared to go into hospital when the psychiatrist suggested this and had made it very clear that he would not be changing his mind on this. All in all, the young man told his medical colleague, he could find no justification for forcing Cyril into hospital. The psychiatrist felt he could not really find fault with this. The ASW reported back to the GP to this effect.

Ten weeks later, June returned to her work in the local CPN team. Even as she was arranging to take over Cyril's case again, the housing officer rang to say that the Council were planning to take their tenant to Court next week in order to evict him; he was now over six months in arrears with his rent. He felt sure that this potential disaster could be avoided if Cyril could be persuaded to go into hospital and accept treatment. Couldn't something be done?

Having first written Cyril a short note to explain she was now back at work, June called round at the flat a couple of days later. She was shocked at the deterioration which had taken place in her client. A slight man at the best of times, Cyril must have lost between two and three stones since she saw him last. He looked at least fifteen years older than he had ten months ago! Cyril gave a little cry as he took his visitor by the arm and pulled her indoors.

June found the flat bereft of all the warm touches it had boasted before; it was bare and, as she quickly discovered, so were the fridge and food cupboard except for a tin of dried milk and a packet of dried potato. When she asked him about this, Cyril told June that he had to save every penny of his pension because he knew he would end up destitute otherwise. He had used no heating in the flat that winter and he bought himself a pie from the corner shop when he was hungry. 'There's no need to have loads of food,' he told June sternly.

When the nurse asked about the rent arrears, Cyril stiffened and became defensive. After a while, he muttered that everyone knew that his parents had paid too much rent all those years; the Council owed him thousands of pounds and the Court would confirm that this was true. When June queried this, he stared at her for a moment and then asked icily, 'why did they bring you back; what are you doing here?' With this, he walked to the door and opened it, telling his old friend to leave and not to come back.

June did call back the next day but she got no further than the doorstep, with Cyril screaming abuse through the letterbox. The nurse went back to the office to talk with her team manager, who in turn called an urgent meeting so that she and June could discuss the pending crisis with the GP and with representatives from the housing and social services departments. At this meeting, it was decided that the situation was now desperate if Cyril was to keep his home; a further mental health assessment was urgently called for.

The mental health assessment took place two days later and an ASW, who was also a social work team leader, called at the flat with Cyril's psychiatrist and his GP. As before, Cyril was civil and invited the professionals inside, reiterating as he did so that he would not be going into hospital. Shortly after they arrived and had talked with their patient for a while, both doctors completed their medical recommendations for Cyril to be admitted to hospital on a six-month section, before they left the ASW to make her assessment.

The social worker later met with the GP and told him that she was not prepared to abuse this man's rights and section him. It was clear that Cyril was hostile and abrasive by nature, but that was not a sign of madness! He was fed up with everyone intruding on his privacy. He was lucid and quite able to explain that he wanted to be left in peace, and why not? When she had asked him about feeding himself, Cyril had shown her a pork pie in the fridge and some packet potato, with the acid comment 'and I should be enjoying this now if you weren't here prying!'. It was very clear that this elderly man dreaded being forced into hospital and the ASW was not prepared to take away his freedom. When the GP protested about his patient's mental and physical condition, the evidence of his poor nutrition and, more urgently, the threat of losing his home and security, the ASW told him that Cyril needed social work support and she would be arranging this for him. The GP reminded her that he and his medical colleague both believed Cyril was psychotic, suffering with delusions about poverty and not paying his rent because he was paranoid about the council and believed they had taken too much rent from his parents. The ASW told him she believed Cyril's problems were social ones and that these could be sorted out in the community. Exasperated, the doctor could not see what else he could do for the old man; it seemed to him that the system sometimes got in the way rather than helped his most vulnerable patients.

Perhaps predictably, the social worker who was allocated to sort out Cyril's problems lasted no longer than a second visit before she was shown the door. Meanwhile, a few weeks later, the housing department, apparently deserted by the other agencies which were meant to be involved with their tenant, finally gave up on a thankless task and Cyril was evicted – literally, physically removed from his home, in the presence of social workers. He was distraught and quite unable to take in what was happening.

The only accommodation social workers could find for him was a homeless people's hostel at the other end of the town, far away from everything Cyril knew. They took him there and helped him unpack. They had reports within a day or so that Cyril had been causing a disturbance, screaming at other residents during the night. By the time they arrived to investigate an hour or so later, Cyril had walked out without a word to anyone.

COMMENT

This is one of those cases which raise so much concern in carers. Cyril's mother feared for her son's well-being after she died and this, of course, is a very common fear. Health professionals are frequently asked by elderly parents 'what will happen when I'm gone?'. Kindly reassurance does not usually relieve their anxiety because all too often they know of cases like Cyril's. This is a great pity because many sufferers show the potential not only to survive but also to find a quite reasonable quality of life after the carer's death, as indeed was the case with Cyril initially. All that may be required for many such sufferers is a modest social network and a measure of planning and continuity of care to ensure a safety-net is immediately available at the first sign of a relapse.

Perhaps you might find it worthwhile to pause for a moment and consider when and why you feel things started to go wrong for Cyril and, that being the case, at which stages opportunities were later missed to protect him from his psychosis?

GROUP'S ANALYSIS OF CASE STUDY

Members of the LEAP group were distressed about the experience of this vulnerable elderly man. They could find plenty of evidence of goodwill and expertise in some of those involved in this case but they also found a frightening lack of understanding about serious mental illness and the needs of its victims.

A friend in need

The group felt that Cyril made a promising start with coping with life after his mother's death and that much of this was due to June, the CPN who took note of the mother's fears for her son's future. 'Yes', a carer commented, 'and she made a jolly good job of supporting him and demonstrated how well some sufferers can cope with a little tender loving care!'

While others in the group heartily agreed with this sentiment, they were concerned that June had not seen a need for others in the system to be involved with Cyril as well as herself. A survivor felt that initially June was exactly what the bereaved man needed but that, later, it would have been useful if she'd used her relationship with Cyril to persuade him to attend a day centre where he could have got to know other sufferers and someone else could have kept an eye on him. Similarly, she felt it would have been a good idea to have arranged for a befriender to call on Cyril regularly, also providing continuity when June had to go away.

Members agreed that either idea would have been much better than leaving Cyril isolated. 'Like the rest of us', someone pointed out, 'he needed a social network and to know that there was always someone out there for him'. 'Yes,' another member agreed, 'and the nurse really should have known she would have to leave Cyril at some time; she could never take the place of family. He'd always need someone else besides her'. As it was, everyone agreed, the poor man had been bereaved once more and June's colleagues seemed to be unaware of this...

A disaster waiting to happen?

'We don't know whether Cyril was pining for June,' a survivor remarked, 'but he was clearly persevering with the new nurse until she let him down: why didn't she warn him she'd be on holiday the next time his injection was due?'

Members agreed this was unfortunate and so was the appearance of two young women, both strangers, at the door, with one of them announcing she had come to give him the injection. However, there was a general feeling that all this was a disaster waiting to happen; Cyril was already very vulnerable and no one seemed to be aware that this was to be expected given the fact that he now really did seem to be completely alone in the world.

A fatal delay?

Members couldn't understand why, when she was turned away, the young nurse didn't do something about this immediately. Why, they wanted to know, couldn't someone else have gone round immediately it was clear that Cyril hadn't had the injection which was due – the team leader, for instance or, perhaps, a male nurse? 'Even ask the GP to call and check that everything was OK?' a carer suggested. 'Yes, do something; anything!', another interjected. As it was, the group felt that the CPN team's reaction two weeks later was too little, too late and remained so until a concerned housing officer intervened.

A first mental health assessment

Members were impressed with the GP's role in this case. It seemed to them that he lost no time at all in seeking help for Cyril, having first made a home visit and also studied his patient's notes. This pleased a survivor who sometimes asks during discussions on case studies, 'doesn't anyone ever read the patient's notes?'

Members were not so impressed with the resulting mental health assessment. It seemed to them that the psychiatrist had just assumed that Cyril was showing the signs of too much stress over the previous few years. 'Why didn't he ask his patient why he was refusing to have his injections or why he was refusing to pay any rent?', a carer wanted to know? 'and why he wouldn't let his own GP over his doorstep?', another asked?

'Well, there's no signs of this and if he did so, he'd certainly have had some difficulty over Cyril's answers I imagine', a survivor remarked thoughtfully, 'and that might have helped the ASW understand what was happening. I really don't believe he did.'

As it was, the group noted that the psychiatrist 'could not really find fault' with the ASW feeling there was no justification for forcing Cyril into hospital. However, members felt that in fact the younger man had very little idea about psychosis or about Cyril's medical history and was content to identify with Cyril's indignation about this intrusion on his privacy. Why, a carer wanted to know, wasn't the social worker interested in practical things such as wanting to check that Cyril had enough food and why it was so cold in the flat that he needed to wear outdoor clothes? 'And why wasn't he concerned either about Cyril's refusing to pay any rent? Did he think that this vulnerable man wouldn't mind losing his home?' a survivor asked.

'In this case, so many "right questions" could have been asked which would have given the game away', groaned a carer. 'Why do I always get the feeling that those involved just want to leave things as they are, not to upset anyone, or uncover any unpleasant truths?' Yes, the group noted, things were left just as they were for another ten weeks.

More delay

'Once again, it took the housing officer to shake everyone into action!' a carer observed, 'isn't it strange that this man put Cyril's behaviour down to mental illness whereas the two professionals who did the mental health assessment weren't able to make the connection?' Indeed, this was a phenomenon which the group had noted while working on *Getting into the System*; the fact that members of the lay public seem to recognize abnormal behaviour in a fellow human being before professionals working with serious mental illness do (1). 'Quite,' agreed a second carer, 'and it's clear that this man felt that Cyril's illness was an adequate explanation for his not paying his rent and that other laymen like council members could, and would, understand that!'

An old friend's return

Members felt that Cyril's initial reaction to June's return confirmed how much he had missed her. 'And his reaction to her queries about the Council owing his parents money demonstrated how quickly he could become paranoid about her too!' a carer pointed out. 'Well, anyway, June and the housing officer between them managed to get everyone to focus their attention on what was happening to Cyril at last,' observed another carer, 'and it seemed they all agreed something must be done urgently, so what went wrong?'

So far as the group could make out, the purpose of the inter-agency meeting was to ensure that all agencies understood the situation, including Cyril's past medical history; his refusal to take medication over the past months; his belief that he didn't have to pay rent and that the court would confirm this; and the evidence of change of behaviour, as confirmed by the housing officer, the GP and now the CPN who knew him so well. 'And, of course, the doctor's notes which confirmed that his behaviour only changed like this when he was ill and that he only became ill when he didn't take his medication', someone pointed out. This had evidently been achieved and led to a decision to call for a second mental health assessment. 'Yes, and not a case conference with the housing department – which would have been the appropriate thing to do if they hadn't all believed Cyril was ill', a survivor observed. So, again, members asked, how did things go wrong at this point?

Second mental health assessment

Members' attention immediately focused on the ASW's role in this assessment, as she appeared to be the only professional involved in the case who did not believe that Cyril needed treatment and protection. One carer said that she would be too angry for words if her family ever met up with a social worker like this again; she had thought that everyone now understood the need for treatment once a sufferer was psychotic after all the horror stories which had hit the headlines over the past few years.

'Yes, I agree', another carer agreed, 'the ASW should have had all the information she needed to recognize that Cyril was not himself; he was not acting as he did when he was well. And she knew that everyone involved with Cyril believed that he should be protected from losing his home as well as getting care and treatment for his illness'.

'Yes', but it seems to me that this woman knew very little about serious mental illness,' a survivor remarked thoughtfully, 'and if that's the case I think I can identify with her seeing Cyril as a vulnerable old man who was being pushed around by her colleague professionals!'

'But surely she could see that he'd be pushed around a lot more if he found himself homeless?' another survivor protested, 'I don't suppose Cyril wanted to be in a homeless people's hostel any more than he wanted to be in hospital! I know I wouldn't ...'

'Well, I have to say that this ASW appeared not to want to do a section anyway; all she could talk about was Cyril's right to stay out of hospital. I thought sectioning was all about overriding that right when sufferers don't believe they're ill and they urgently need help!', exclaimed a carer.

'Yes, I agree with you,' another carer joined in, 'The ASW must have ignored all the incidents and concerns of others over the past months, not to mention Cyril's previous medical history, and the recommendations of the two doctors'. And most of all, she ignored the risks of him losing his home and what that would mean for his future. She should have taken all this into account before considering whether or not to section him and I don't see how she could have done.' (2)

No one had any argument with this and members decided to take a more detailed look at the role of ASWs in their work with serious mental illness in their later discussion.

THE WIDER PERSPECTIVE

At this point, the LEAP group went on to consider several issues in this case which concerned them:

A special relationship

Members touched on this subject earlier when they were discussing June's leaving to go on a course. There was a general feeling that this nurse provided the sort of support which most sufferers and their families would really appreciate. But they felt that as she had been the only person in Cyril's life since his mother died, he might very well have become dependent upon her. Some members were quick to point out that Cyril's diagnosis might make this more likely as it is not unusual for sufferers to prefer to relate on a 'one to one' basis and, when not really well, to relate to just one person and to regard all others as intruders on this relationship.

One carer explained, 'My son's like that – it makes things difficult when he gets ill because no one else gets a look in; he follows me around the house and snarls at other members of the family. Yet when he's well again, I'm not particularly important; he's closer to his brother normally'.

'And when you say he follows you around, you mean he even hovers on the landing if you go to the toilet or have a bath? That's how it is with my son: it's the first sign he's relapsing', agreed another member.

'Yes', grinned a survivor, 'and in the 1960s and 1970s when the family theories flourished (3), then this clinging relationship was viewed as very suspect on the mother's part, you know!' (4)

'Whereas', someone else pointed out, 'everyone can see that this special relationship can be with the mother or a girlfriend, a tutor, a social worker or a nurse, as might have been the case with Cyril'. 'Yes, but Cyril had no one else anyway and we all need someone', a survivor pointed out. 'June really should have taken account of this.' Members agreed and noted that if Cyril was totally dependent upon the nurse he went to a lot of trouble to hide it from her. Everyone agreed that, either way, at least two workers, preferably from different agencies, should be involved with sufferers who have no family to support them.

Members were very sure that continuity of care was vitally important for someone with a serious mental illness. They felt that Cyril's case demonstrated this well and that if someone else had been involved with him then June's departure wouldn't have left him so vulnerable. They felt that a second worker could have acted as an advocate for him when this mattered; for example, when he turned away the young nurse who was a stranger to him.

The importance of medication

This brought members to the point where they felt the rot set in for Cyril; the point at which he refused his injection and, more importantly, no one followed this up immediately. The group has found again and again that the system doesn't respond urgently to news that a sufferer has missed taking tablets or having an injection. One member of the group, quoted earlier on this same subject in Chapter 2, could not understand why professionals don't appreciate the importance of acting quickly at this crucial stage. As he pointed out, 'time is short – it need only be a matter of a day or two before the sufferer will refuse to take the medication'. He felt sure that there really was a case for more effective education for professionals on the role of medication in a serious mental illness. 'After all', he concluded, 'people on medication don't usually become miraculously well when the medication is stopped!'.

As we noted in Chapter 2, the importance of appropriate medication in a serious mental illness is something which particularly concerns the LEAP group because it applies so much to the very sufferers who can be well enough to get on with their lives, as Cyril was starting to do before June left. Some of these 'acute' sufferers are even well enough to hold down important and responsible jobs, staying well as long as they are prepared to persevere with taking medication. Because everyone in the LEAP group has experienced acute psychotic illness personally or has lived with it, its members are very conscious that it is medication which controls the chemical imbalance which can otherwise ruin a sufferer's life.

As a survivor pointed out, 'In this, our problems are very similar to diabetic sufferers who need to take Insulin regularly – except, of course, those around them are more conscious of the dangers in diabetes because death may be more predictable and immediate!' (5)

Another survivor summed up the group's feelings on this matter with 'everything would be so much easier if only professionals could understand that some of us, if we always take medication, can get well enough to do without the system most of the time. It's only when things go wrong that we need them, and our medication, quickly!'

'Yes,' agreed another member who has suffered relapses herself, 'and we won't seem raving mad when we desperately need help – that is, unless they leave us too long and we risk losing everything that matters to us'.

'Right, but it seems to me that this is where everything can go wrong for the likes of us' someone else pointed out, 'look at what the ASW said about Cyril: that he was abrasive and hostile by nature. Having decided that, she went straight off down the wrong track, didn't she? This happened to me too during my last breakdown. ASWs – and other professionals, come to that – decided it was my usual way to be hostile and domineering, so they shut their ears to what my family and friends had to say!' She glanced round the group, adding 'it is scary, isn't it? All the evidence was there that my personality had changed beyond recognition, but I wasn't "running mad", you see!'

This point in the discussion brought the group back to the vexing question of how the law is used, or not, as the case may be, when someone's serious mental illness threatens to destroy them.

A question of attitude?

When the group analyzed Cyril's second mental health assessment, we noted that one carer was exasperated to find that some social workers still disregarded, or were ignorant about, the dangers of an untreated psychosis. While other members sympathized with this viewpoint, they were equally concerned with this particular ASW's preoccupation with protecting the sufferer from being forced into hospital rather than adhering to the role defined and described in her professional guidelines. In particular, they referred to the requirement for the ASW to listen to the opinions and experiences of those who know the sufferer in normal circumstances and in particular other involved professionals and family. Nevertheless, when they returned to this subject now, a survivor intervened with 'Yes, but ASWs have to make up their own mind about whether or not someone needs sectioning, and that's only right, I suppose'.

'Yes', agreed another member, 'and I do think we should bear in mind that some of them must be "anti" hospitals in general when they hear what some sufferers have to say about their treatment when they've been sectioned. I certainly wouldn't want anyone to experience what happened to me – having a needle forced into me with five nurses holding me down. I know I was unlucky, but I still shudder when I think of it! Perhaps social workers only hear the bad news, and incidents like mine, and then decide they're not going to be any part of it – unless of course the sufferer's raving mad and there's no other answer'.

'Yes, I can see that,' another survivor joined in thoughtfully, 'but if that's the case, then those social workers should do some other work; they aren't there to exercise their political views, are they?' 'They're there to decide whether or not someone's needs can be catered for properly outside of hospital.'

Another survivor agreed and said she felt it was a great pity that ASWs were probably biased about serious mental illness and about its treatment, perhaps because of their training? Those social workers she knew talked about 'scapegoating', 'labelling' and 'putting people away' rather than about 'treatment' and 'care' and getting people well again. 'I don't believe they realize', she added, 'that getting into hospital under section can be your one chance of survival once it happens to you!'. She may be right; 5 years after the 70 days of ASW training came into operation, a survey revealed that newly trained ASWs felt they didn't know enough about the mentally ill and matters concerning the mentally ill (6).

'Yes', a previous speaker came back, 'I can't forget what happened to me when I was in hospital but I always weigh that against the fact that I came out the other end and now I don't see how anyone can deny a sufferer that opportunity, I don't really'.

ASWs – an absolute power?

Although most members of the LEAP group were quite prepared to accept that the second ASW in Cyril's case may have been well-meaning and genuinely concerned with complying with his wishes not to go into hospital, they had little doubt that her approach to this assessment had not been professional. They found this very worrying as it seemed that there was nothing her colleagues could do about her decision although the GP tried by carefully explaining the state of Cyril's mental health, the change in his usual behaviour and why he was refusing to pay his rent. A survivor observed that, for her, this was a very definite failure of the system; 'too often', she explained, 'the individuals who have to make a decision about whether or not sectioning is called for are the very ones who don't know the sufferer! For example', she added, 'in Cyril's case, there were doctors and nurses who knew him before he relapsed and they realized he was mentally and physically unwell. Yet another professional who had never met him before can come in and decide they are all wrong and the law shouldn't be used to get their patient into hospital.'

Other members agreed that this seemed very odd; given that a sufferer was not literally running amok, then they believed the only real way they could be assessed was by measuring the *change which had taken place in their normal personality and behaviour.* They couldn't see how a stranger could do that.

A need for a nearest relative?

Someone pointed out now that in Chapter 2 the group had considered the nearest relative's right to apply for a section if an ASW refused to do so. It seemed to him that, so long as the nearest relative knew of this right, this provided a balance – a safety-net at this crucial stage in a crisis. However, Cyril didn't have any relatives left to fight for him, did he?

'That's right,' replied a survivor, 'so the ASW was in charge in every sense of the word and I can't believe this was what was intended when the law was made'. Other members agreed; it seemed to them that Cyril had been the victim of an anomaly in the law. However, a carer who has taken part in social working training courses pointed out that the Mental Health Act allowed for any person to be appointed as a nearest relative in the County Court. When they heard this, members felt that this should have been sorted out for Cyril, either at the time of his mother's death or at the first sign of a need to think about using the law.

Or more of the same?

Members realized that after a short time a third mental health assessment could have been arranged, if the sufferer could stand the continued stress of professionals calling to assess him, and, of course, they could have found him! 'But this sort of carry-on makes no sense in humane or economic terms, does it?' protested a carer. No, everyone agreed, it didn't!

A need for change?

The LEAP group had no doubt that mental health assessments should be all about listening and learning, together with liaison between all those involved. It should not, they insisted, be a situation in which a newcomer can defy the received wisdom of everyone else involved and not be accountable for doing so. What could be done about this loophole in the law, they wanted to know?

This question brought a swift reaction from one of the younger survivors in the group, who is the first to acknowledge that she has had good experiences with social workers. 'I don't believe that ASWs should have the power to block everyone,' she declared, 'but I'd go further than that. In my experience, doctors, CPNs and relatives usually know what they're doing because they know the sufferer and they know about serious mental illness. Why do social workers have to be involved in the sectioning process? Why can't we have more of them supporting sufferers and carers out in the community, instead?'

A carer who has spent many years supporting families as well as working with sufferers seemed to sum up the exasperation of her fellow members with her response to the previous speaker, 'Yes, when it comes to using the law, ASWs have power over the professionals who have the contact with sufferers and know how ill they really are', she agreed. 'I think there has to be a change of procedure; otherwise I can't see how things will ever change. We have seen situations like this time and time again'.

SUMMING UP

Members felt this was a particularly sad case and their concerns with Cyril's story focused on (a) the need for an adequate social network for sufferers who don't have a family to support them, (b) the importance of medication in acute psychotic illness and, most of all, (c) the unique power of ASWs to choose whether or not the law should be used in order to provide treatment and protection for an individual with a serious mental illness.

INFORMATION

The following pieces of information are relevant to points brought up in the group's analysis and discussion which have been highlighted in the text:

(1) Why do the lay people seem to recognize abnormal behaviour more easily than professionals working with serious mental illness?

During the LEAP group's work on Chapter 5 in *Getting into the System* (the first book in this series), members noted the fact that lay members of the public – such as family, friends, neighbours, shop-keepers and work colleagues – frequently recognize serious mental illness in a sufferer before mental health professionals appear to do so. In view of the acknowledged dangers of delaying treatment in a psychotic illness, they decided that the exercise at the end of that chapter should be based on the following question: Is it possible that the professional training and day-to-day experience of those who work with serious mental illness might prejudice their natural skills in recognizing abnormal behaviour in another human being?

---

(2) Mental health assessments – what to look for

The *Code of Practice* discusses in detail the factors which should be taken into consideration when assessing whether or not a sufferer needs to be admitted under the Act. (See pp. 4–6)

(3) The family theories of schizophrenia

During the 1960s and 1970s there was an abundance of theories of a similar ilk which blamed the families of schizophrenia sufferers for their relative's illness. These dominated much of the literature and received wisdom of the time and added significantly to the misery of families trying to cope with living with a serious mental illness.

Long since discredited, because, among other things, it turned out that researchers were discovering for the first time the idiosyncrasies of normal family life rather than anything unusual about families coping with schizophrenia, they have nevertheless influenced for many years the attitudes of some of those who in turn have influence over the training of recruits to the caring professions.

For a full discussion and useful references on this subject, see *The Reality of Schizophrenia*, Faber & Faber, 1991, (pp. 79–81) by the author.

(4) A clinging relationship

This sort of dependent relationship – usually with the mother – is at its most intense at times when the sufferer is most vulnerable; that is, the period leading up to breakdown and throughout an acute episode of schizophrenia – and was therefore something which professionals frequently first noted in families in crisis. This was seen as yet one more visible feature of possessive, suffocating mothering at a time when the expression schizophrenogenic mother (jargon of the day for mothers who were believed to cause schizophrenia in their offspring – they were variously described as being cold, too emotional, too distant, over-involved, possessive, too domineering, or too submissive) was a frequently used phrase in psychiatry. It escaped notice that, in general, the mothers were initially shocked and disturbed by their grown offspring's sudden regression to the dependence of young childhood. Later, like the two mothers in LEAP group who talked about this phenomenon, families came to recognize that the chosen person was nothing more or less than a life-line during an illness which inflicts devastating confusion and isolation on its victims.

(5) Comparison with diabetes

Back in the 1970s, Kety, a leading psychiatrist in the USA, pointed out that diabetes mellitus was analogous to schizophrenia in many ways. 'Both are symptom clusters or syndromes...Each may have many aetiologies and show a range of intensity from severe and debilitating to latent or borderline. There is also evidence that genetic and environmental influences operate in the development of both' ('From rationalization to reason', *American Journal of Psychiatry 131*, 9, September 1974 p. 962)

Increasingly, psychiatrists in this country point out similarities in the two conditions, also emphasizing that many schizophrenia sufferers have to accept a need to take neuroleptic medication indefinitely for their chemical imbalance in the same way that many diabetes sufferers have to accept a need to take Insulin every day.

(6) ASW training

CCETSW Paper No 19.25, 'Refresher Training for Approved Social Workers', February 1990, reported that ASWs did not feel they knew enough about the mentally ill and matters concerning the mentally ill.

Families frequently report that these social workers, whom they see as specialists working with serious mental illness, do not seem to understand about living with such an illness and what a psychotic crisis is all about. This does not seem to be a fair or reasonable situation for either party.

EXERCISE

Imagine you have been asked by the Department of Health to find a way of remedying the seemingly absolute power of the ASW in cases such as Cyril's, without changing the existing mental health legislation.

Detail your recommendations and illustrate how these should have led to a more democratic and rewarding outcome in this particular case.

CHAPTER 5

Slipping into the wrong system

When professionals working with the mental health legislation are not fully conversant with their powers or are reluctant to use them, then increasingly there is a risk that sufferers will slip into the criminal system. Let's take a look at what happened to Dave.

CASE STUDY

When he was 30 years of age and had been married for no more than a few months, Dave suffered a breakdown and his GP treated him for a 'mild psychotic episode'. This coincided with a recession and Dave finding himself out of work for the first time since he had obtained an apprenticeship in carpentry when he left school. The doctor explained that his illness was a reaction to stress and prescribed neuroleptic medication, suggesting that he come to the surgery for monthly prescriptions for the time being.

Dave soon felt better and confident enough to go and look for work. Because he was a mild and agreeable man who had proved himself to be a gifted craftsman, his former employer was happy to give Dave a good reference and it was not long before he found another job. Within three months or so of starting this, Dave became more and more reluctant to persevere with the medication, particularly as he and his wife both suspected that this was the cause of his feeling tired all the time. His doctor, however, suggested he should only reduce the dose gradually so that he could monitor his progress.

In the event, Dave was so confident that he was well again that he didn't bother to go back the following month for his prescription. He was rewarded very quickly by a burst of energy and feeling more like he used to before he became ill. Moreover, his parents and his in-laws noticed the difference in him and everyone sighed with relief that this unfortunate episode was over and felt that it had obviously been caused by the stress of losing his job.

However, it was not long before Dave started to feel insecure again. Although his new employer was putting off men who had been with the firm longer than him, Dave nevertheless began to suspect that there was a conspiracy to get rid of him too. He was so sure that this was the case that he confronted his boss several times over the next few weeks, demanding reassurance that he was not about to be sacked. Although the older man was surprised, he was good natured enough to point out that he rarely came across the sort of skills he'd noted in Dave, so he certainly did not want to lose him.

Dave's wife quickly sensed that something was going wrong. Dave seemed to be suspicious and agitated a lot of the time and never stopped complaining about his new boss. Things quickly deteriorated and, far from being tired and sleepy as before, Dave was pacing the floor all night and continuing to pester his boss about the security of his job during the day. The man was beginning to find his new employee's manner quite threatening and he was anyway losing patience with his demands for reassurance. Also, Dave had started arriving late for work in the mornings looking as if he had had no sleep and his work was suffering. Very soon, Dave's fears about losing his job became a self-fulfilling prophecy and he found himself unemployed again.

Things started to get worse with Dave retreating to his bed during the daytime and pacing round the house all night. It was another ten weeks before his wife eventually managed to persuade Dave to see the GP and by this time she was past caring about their marriage or their home, which the building society was anyway threatening to repossess. The doctor lost no time in arranging for a psychiatrist to call at the home and the specialist put Dave back on the medication which had helped him before, telling him that he really must persevere with this; he had a schizophrenic illness. Once back on the medication, Dave quickly became well again but it was too late to save his marriage or his home.

Initially shattered, Dave gradually came to terms with what had happened and resumed living with his parents who had recently bought a bungalow 16 miles away from their old home. This meant a change of GP and psychiatrist for Dave, both of whom met their new patient for the first time when he was virtually his old self again. Before very long, the specialist reduced his medication quite substantially as Dave complained he was completely lacking in energy and said that the drugs made him feel sleepy and too tired to consider finding work.

Within a couple of weeks of the medication being reduced, Dave once more decided he didn't need to take it any longer; he was feeling so much better now. With this new burst of energy, he was beginning to find his confidence again and he started looking for work. However, a couple of weeks later, Dave told his mother that he realized that no one would employ him and muttered something about this being due to his father. She couldn't make any sense of what he was saying but she did note that just lately he seemed to be rather moody and grumpy, quite unlike his normally mild and agreeable self.

The next morning, Dave started cursing and shouting at his father. His parents had never seen him behave this way before and were at a loss to understand what had caused this outburst. Later in the day, with a truly amazing show of strength, Dave tore down the garden shed he had painstakingly built for the older man when his parents had moved into their new home. They were devastated and immediately rang the GP for help. As Dave refused to see him, the doctor arranged for a CPN to make an urgent visit to the home and the nurse arrived a few hours later.

The CPN was alarmed at the tension he found in Dave and in the home. He sensed that the father was very nervous and suggested that the older man should accompany him to the gate. The nurse then learned that Dave had had his hands round his father's throat the previous night and that he believed that it was only his wife's terrified cries that had stopped his son seriously hurting him. Could the nurse do something quickly before anything else happened, he wanted to know?

The CPN reported back to the doctor that he believed the situation called for an urgent mental health assessment and early that evening the GP, a psychiatrist and an ASW called at the home. They didn't stay very long because Dave made it very clear he didn't want to talk to them and after ten minutes or so he suddenly got up, saying 'that's it' and went to his room. When they left, the social worker told the parents that they felt nothing could be done at the moment; Dave didn't seem to be sectionable at this time. His mother pointed out that Dave had torn down a good garden shed as if it was made of paper yesterday morning and nearly throttled his father that evening; what more did they need to know? She was told that if Dave became violent again, then they should call the police.

The CPN was so concerned by the situation he found when he called at the home the next morning that he asked one of his colleagues to join him when he went back to see the family later in the day. Both nurses immediately reported their urgent concern to the GP and to the local social work team. The following day, a second mental health assessment was carried out by the GP and a different ASW, together with the psychiatrist who had reduced Dave's medication and who would continue to supervise his treatment. This time, Dave stayed throughout the professionals' visit and he seemed subdued but quite coherent. He complained there had been nothing but trouble since he took down a shed because he was not satisfied with it. He was fed up with his parents whingeing about this and he found their fussing all the time a real hassle. Once again, the elderly couple were told that Dave was showing no signs of being sectionable and the psychiatrist suggested to the parents 'I think you should back off a little and give your son some space'. Again, the mother followed the visitors to the door and pleaded with them to do something and again she was told that if Dave showed any further signs of violence, they should call the police. When the father queried this, almost hysterical, it was explained that once he had been arrested, then the doctors would be able to get their son into hospital more easily.

For a day or two, things quietened down and Dave spent most of his time in his room. However, on the third day, he stormed into the lounge where his parents were watching the nine o'clock news and started shouting at his father again. His mother left the room and immediately telephoned the GP's surgery and, much to her relief, a locum doctor arrived very quickly and went off with Dave to talk with him alone. Ten minutes later, the doctor came back to the parents and told them that this so-called emergency was nothing more than a personality clash between son and father. He did not expect to be called out in such circumstances. The astonished parents had scarcely opened their mouths in protest before he had gone.

The doctor's visit appeared to have calmed Dave down and his parents waited anxiously until he went off to his room. Several hours later, still sitting tense and nervous by the now blank television, they were startled by a door banging. Seconds later, Dave stormed into the room, threatening his father again and starting to destroy any of his possessions which came to hand. Terrified, his mother called the police. As they arrived, Dave threw his father several feet and he caught his head on the wall as he fell. He agreed to charge his son, as the mental health professionals had previously advised, and explained to the police that Dave had a mental illness and he and his wife wanted him to receive the treatment that had made him well before. The police were sympathetic when they heard how the parents had been trying to get help for Dave and told them that their son would be transferred to hospital if he was mentally ill. Meanwhile, he would be taken to a prison 30 miles away. The parents were stunned; they couldn't believe that all their efforts to get help for their son had resulted in this.

They will never forget the weeks that followed. As they continued to plead that Dave was mentally ill, so they were told by a probation worker that it seemed there were no signs of this. The CPNs tried to reassure the couple and both nurses did what they could to urge that some action should be taken before Dave, still without medication, was tempted to harm himself or others and make matters worse than they already were. As it happened, the doctor had to make two 60-mile round trips to the prison and produce two court reports before Dave's transfer to hospital was achieved.

By the time he was discharged from hospital three months later, Dave was stabilized on a depot injection and his parents were reassured by this. However, several years on, he has never had the confidence to take up work again and he spends most of his time in the bungalow, bored and restless. Meanwhile, he frequently dreams he is back in the prison again, waking up distressed.

Dave's parents remain grateful to this day for the sensitivity the police showed their troubled son and for intervening on his first appearance in court when a shocked magistrate wanted to send this vulnerable man straight home. They kept in touch with the family until Dave was safely in hospital. Similarly, the parents cannot praise too highly the efforts made by the CPNs to get help for their son and for their support during the weeks after his arrest. However, they cannot forgive the professionals who turned their backs on their son, nor can they forgive themselves for taking their 'expert' advice. As Dave's mother explains, 'the trauma of prison for a sick, vulnerable person and the parents having put him there never goes away'.

COMMENT

There is a striking similarity in Dave's case to the experiences of Kim and Cyril in earlier chapters of this book in that they all slipped out of the mental health system despite having a diagnosis of serious mental illness and although they had been subjected to at least two mental health assessments, involving several different professionals working with the law. However, Dave's case is particularly worrying in one aspect: it would seem that the professionals who assessed him 'passed the buck' – and their patient – to a system not intended for, nor equipped to cope with, the seriously mentally ill. This seems to be a serious failure in a costly system set up to treat and care for the mentally ill.

It might be useful to pause at this point before going on to read the group's discussion on this case study. Perhaps you might like to make a note of any features in this case which you believe may have led to Dave not receiving more appropriate help for his psychotic crisis, and to make comments on each of these as you do so?

LEAP GROUP'S ANALYSIS OF THE CASE STUDY

Not surprisingly, LEAP group members were distressed that Dave could land up in prison when his behaviour and previous medical history clearly called for the use of the mental health legislation to protect him and his father from the effects of his serious mental illness. They were at a loss to understand why the professionals who had the power to use the Mental Health Act did not do so but instead gave the family advice which led to the sufferer being taken to prison. Because of this the group decided to focus particularly on this aspect of Dave's case during the analysis which follows.

First two breakdowns

Members noted that his GP had successfully treated Dave's first psychotic episode in the community rather than having him admitted to hospital. It seemed to them that the only problem with this may have been that it minimized his illness in the eyes of his wife and the rest of the family. Either way, Dave, in common with many sufferers known to the group, came out of his first psychotic episode without understanding either the role of the medication or his potential vulnerability to become ill again. One member was adamant that 'This is why it is so important to make sure that the sufferer understands about his illness and the reason for taking the medication. I was lucky; all this was explained to me. I certainly would not have put up with the side effects I had initially otherwise!'

Members agreed that Dave had responded well to medication and the doctor had wisely cautioned his patient to persevere with this. However, a carer, who has shown concern over this matter in the past, pointed out, 'once again, it seems that there was no follow up when the patient didn't turn up for his monthly prescription'. The group felt this was a valid criticism; since doctors are well aware that sufferers tend to reject the medication, it seemed unreasonable that it should be one of their priorities to monitor their progress and follow up any missed appointments.

Members felt that a more significant omission was the lack of explanations given to Dave and his family. They knew that doctors often avoid 'labelling' a patient with a stigmatizing diagnosis such as schizophrenia but they insisted that it was more important to ensure that they obtain insight into their illness and an understanding of their own vulnerability. Also, as one member commented, 'Dave's wife might not have given up on her marriage so quickly if she'd had a chance to understand what was happening to him'. 'Yes', someone agreed, 'and she would, no doubt, have encouraged Dave not to give up on his medication'.

The group did feel that the lack of proper explanations was very relevant to the outcome of Dave's illness; his response to the medication following his first two breakdowns did suggest that there was every chance that he could have avoided relapse and gradually become more well if he had fully understood why it was so important to keep on taking it. 'Instead, the treatment amounted to little more than first-aid each time, and eventually resulted in this serious crisis', someone concluded.

A predictable third breakdown?

Members were concerned about the poor communication and lack of continuity which often seem to be evident when a sufferer moves from one district to another. By this time there was ample evidence that Dave would not comply with taking medication if he could help it but a new psychiatrist was either unaware of this or ignored it. 'But, why?' asked an exasperated survivor, 'Why couldn't he reduce the medication very slightly so that he could monitor its effects on Dave himself?'. Yes, others in the group agreed with her, and, another survivor suggested 'Wouldn't it have been more to the point to have shown an interest in whether or not his tiredness was an unacceptable side effect of the medication or a symptom still hanging around from his breakdown? This might have led to a positive change instead of a disaster!'.

First mental health assessment

The group was glad to note that the GP and CPN both responded quickly to the parents' plea for help and that the CPN went out of his way to find out what was really going on in this home and reported back on this immediately. However, it seemed to them that from this point on it was downhill all the way, starting with the first mental health assessment.

No one could understand how the reports of the parents and the CPN could be ignored because the sufferer had not displayed any unusual behaviour in the short time he remained in the interview with the professionals. As someone pointed out, 'his getting up and leaving them so abruptly should have confirmed just how tense and anxious he was feeling'. Others agreed that Dave's quick departure should have lent more credence to what the CPN and the parents were saying, not less. A carer asked, 'Can someone explain why these professionals shouldn't listen to what another professional was saying? Did they think the nurse had nothing better to do than to rush around trying to get help for this family?' A survivor agreed, 'Yes, we know carers' opinions are often ignored but here is what we've already seen in Kim's and Cyril's cases: a CPN's opinion being ignored too'.

Another relative thought that perhaps the professionals carrying out the assessment didn't want to hear what anyone had to say anyway, because 'they didn't seem to take advantage of Dave's absence to talk with the parents and the poor mother had to rush after them to the door and point out that Dave had pulled down the garden shed and then nearly choked her husband'. 'Yes,' someone added, 'and their reply was rather suspect, wasn't it? Instead of asking her to tell them more about it, or to get in touch with them if it occurred again, they told her to call the police!'

It was this aspect of this case which seriously concerned the LEAP group members. On the one hand, it seemed that the professionals carrying out the assessment had no concerns about the sufferer's behaviour although they had been told he had attacked his father the previous night. On the other hand, the same professionals advised the mother to call the police if there was any further violence.

Second mental health assessment

The group noted that by the time this second assessment took place, those carrying it out were aware that a second nurse was equally concerned about this situation.

This time, Dave hadn't walked out during the assessment. He was subdued, apart from showing irritation over the fuss that had been made about his pulling down a shed; he'd said he was fed up with his parents' whingeing about this. Members of the group noted that seemed to be the end of the matter; no one followed this up and asked him why he had been so angry with his father, threatening and even being violent towards him. As one mother put it, 'Surely they owed that to this Dad? The poor man was in danger, for heavens sake!' Yes, the group found it very hard to accept that this aspect of Dave's crisis seemingly received so little attention.

The group's attention then focused on the last comment made by the professionals when they were leaving; that if Dave was arrested then doctors would be able to get him into hospital more easily. Members felt this was not only nonsense but it was seriously worrying in that any perceived problems with obtaining a bed for a sufferer had no place in a mental health assessment and professionals working with the law should have been well aware of this. And for whom would it be 'easier'? Certainly not for Dave and his family; nor for the rest of this particular psychiatrist's patients as it was clear that a considerable amount of his time was spent on two abortive mental health assessments and then making two trips to a prison thirty miles away and preparing a report each time for the Court!

At this stage, a survivor commented that this case demonstrated a lack of care that she found chilling, adding, 'there seemed to be no concern with the father's safety or with Dave's future – what are these people doing working with serious mental illness?' This comment seemed to sum up the group's feelings about these two mental health assessments and the professionals involved in them.

A last-ditch attempt to get help

Members were further exasperated by the locum's response to the parents' next call for help. This was further evidence, they noted, that some health professionals have no understanding at all of psychotic behaviour and therefore have no way of recognizing it when they meet up with it. Clearly, they felt, the locum was prepared to help; he had responded and come round to the home very quickly. However, he had no appreciation that a frightened sufferer could be lucid in psychosis and successfully project his problems onto those closest to him. Moreover, the doctor apparently saw no need to check further with these parents about the reasons for their agitation. 'I find his behaviour judgmental and extremely discourteous', concluded one carer, 'and once again, the system failed this family and left Dave and his parents exposed to danger and to prolonged misery later on!'

Police intervention

Members were impressed, but not surprised, that the police handled the inevitable crisis in a way that had left the family feeling grateful to them for so long after the crisis was over. This is not an uncommon occurrence (1). At this stage, however, they were more concerned to note that there could have been a fatal tragedy if the police had not arrived so promptly. All agreed that this possibility had been there for all to see and they found it very worrying that only the CPNs had acknowledged this and as one member pointed out, 'They were the only health professionals involved in this crisis who didn't have the power to use the law!'

'Yes, and it wasn't as if the others objected to the law being used; so long as they didn't have to be the ones who did the dirty work!', exclaimed another.

Perhaps this was fair comment. Certainly, no one in the group could make head nor tail of this willingness to 'nudge' Dave into another system; one which was intended for criminals and which could only be used once a crisis had taken place. However, a mother whose family has been left more than once to deal with this sort of dangerous situation on their own, asked quietly, 'Is it possible that some professionals go out of their way to avoid a violent situation? Is it that they're frightened the threatened violence will turn on them, so they leave well alone?'. Interestingly, it turned out that several members had wondered about this in the past, particularly those who had been left 'to get on with it ourselves', as they put it. However, they had tended to dismiss the idea as ridiculous; if it was OK for them to cope on their own 24 hours a day until the crisis was resolved, how could professionals, with all the support they had available to them, be worried about their involvement for anything up to an hour or so? However, they thought about it some more now that the matter had been aired and, because no other explanations seemed to be forthcoming, they decided to take another look at this later.

The aftermath of a crisis

Members could identify with Dave's parents during their agonized wait for his transfer to hospital. They noted that the CPNs still pursued the matter until they were sure that Dave's interests were being protected and that the police officers continued to give the family support during this traumatic period too. However, a survivor pointed out that 'those who should have assessed Dave properly and either used the law or taken other steps to protect him were the ones who apparently offered the family nothing'. Another member who has experienced a psychotic breakdown herself commented, 'Yes, the family were lucky that some of the professionals continued to campaign for the right result. Without this, I fear the prison stay could have been longer'. After a pause, she continued, 'the outcome for Dave is sadly a life where he may never realize his full potential. Some professionals seem satisfied with this sort of result but it can be due to their failures'. No one argued with this summing up of the service provided for Dave and his family.

THE WIDER PERSPECTIVE

As we have noted during their analysis, members of the group discussed various features in this case study which they felt were unresolved. At this point, they went on to look at each of these from a more general viewpoint, starting with the two assessments they found so worrying.

Mental health assessments

It was noticeable that the group had referred to the need to be 'responsible' again and again when they talked earlier about the two assessments in this case and now one carer was clear that the system failed Dave when the assessors did not take a responsible approach to the assessment. He pointed out this included 'finding out how the sufferer usually behaves, looking at the long-term case history, checking out the usual course of that individual's illness and listening to what others close to the sufferer are saying at the time, particularly if there is any risk involved. This is what is required and what should achieve a proper result.' (2)

Bearing in mind the apparent futility of these two mental health assessments and also those carried out on Cyril (see Chapter 4) and, latterly, on Kim (see Chapter 2), the group came to the conclusion that it might be appropriate for those carrying out a mental health assessment to be required to work through a checklist of duties which should be involved in this, and afterwards to explain in writing how they believed the assessment had contributed towards meeting the immediate needs of the sufferer. This, they hoped, would complement their suggestions in Chapter 2 about ensuring that mental health assessments contribute something to the resolving of a crisis.

Passing the buck

The group were in no doubt that professionals who should have been using the mental health law available to them to protect Dave and his family chose instead 'to pass the buck'. As they saw it, telling the family to call the police was certainly passing the buck. As one mother put it, 'it seems to me they were relying on the police to do their work for them', and another carer agreed; 'Yes, they left someone else to take away Dave's liberty and, dare I say, to find him a bed?'. Another member felt that 'it's a waste of police time having to step in because the mental health professionals have mismanaged the situation' and, once again, members concerned themselves with the amount of time and professional skills which were wasted on this case without even serving Dave's interests.

One mother pointed out that when her son relapsed a couple of years ago, she was told by two different ASWs to call the police and when she queried this the second time she got the answer 'in case there's any violence'. She could quite understand why so many sufferers landed up in the criminal system and agreed with a survivor that reading reports in the press saying things like 'this former psychiatric patient has been arrested for ...' were very frightening indeed.

Members had strong opinions about this 'passing of the buck' when this could mean you landing up in the criminal system although your only crime was to have a serious mental illness. They also found it rather at odds with the protests of so many professionals that they didn't want to abuse a patient's rights. Surely, they wanted to know, wasn't one of the most important of those rights to be recognized as having an illness and to be given treatment for this before a disaster could happen? 'And another important right', a survivor protested, 'is to not be treated as a criminal because you're ill!'

Going to prison

Understandably, members felt strongly about a situation in which the neglect of a psychotic crisis could lead to a sufferer going to prison. One of the younger survivors in the group asked, 'don't they realize how frightening it is for the rest of us that a sufferer can go to prison and their families are quite helpless to do anything about it?' Another survivor agreed that this was a nightmare and pointed out that being shut in a prison cell does no one any good, but it could be hell for a sufferer, particularly if medical care was not available. A third survivor summed up this vexed subject with, 'Yes, I find it very, very frightening that someone can be left to become violent when they're psychotic and then have to suffer the consequences'.

Carers were seriously worried too about sufferers like Dave going to prison. One mother said that parents like herself now feared that if a similar event happened in their family, then prison would be the outcome; it was bad enough having to cope with dangerous situations when a crisis occurred without having nightmares about this new threat. Members wondered if the public knew this could happen. They knew other families like Dave's who had found themselves visiting their relatives in prison; something which was as foreign to them as it would be to any of their friends, neighbours or colleagues, 'and as unlikely – until the recent advent of community care', a relative remarked bleakly.

Members found this whole subject particularly sobering because some of them were aware, as one carer pointed out, that an almost unspeakable tragedy had taken place three years earlier in a nearby prison where two sufferers, just admitted on remand, had been put into a cell together and one had been killed by the other in horrendous circumstances (3).

'And yet', exclaimed a carer, 'we are still advised to call the police when we ask mental health professionals for help!'

This last comment brought the group round full circle – why, oh, why, members wanted to know, did some mental health professionals want to pass the buck; even if this meant off-loading someone who was seriously ill onto the criminal system? 'Is it possible they could be unmoved by such a tragedy?' the same mother asked, 'Are they really unable to identify with other human beings who find themselves going down that road?'

A need to distance oneself?

This question 'rang a bell' for another carer in the group. After having to cope with countless crisis situations, it seemed to her that professionals never asked each other, 'Can she manage on her own while we sort out what we can do?' Despite having been known to be in danger on several occasions, this member explained she had been expected to wait – alone – with the sufferer until it was convenient for professionals to come and do an assessment. 'On one occasion', she told us, 'I trekked round with my relative all day: she was restless and determined to be out and about. I felt safer that way too, I suppose. We were passed from one agency to another, while she became more and more tense. We were finally told to go straight to the hospital; once there I had no sooner sank back in a chair with a sigh of relief when the doctor came back with my relative and asked me to take her home and wait for someone to come and see us the next day!' At such times, she went on, she knew for certain that not one of those working with serious mental illness had the vaguest idea what it was like to be alone with someone when they're raging psychotic. 'I do, she concluded, and I wouldn't knowingly inflict it on anyone'.

A survivor agreed, 'You're right – they don't know – they distance themselves from it all'. Members thought about this and finally agreed that this might explain some of the confusing features in cases like Dave's and Kim's and similar ones known to them; instead of being duty-bound to resolve a crisis for a family urgently seeking help, professionals could, if they wanted, distance themselves from the situation with the help of cumbersome procedures and longstanding, ambivalent, civil liberty issues.

The group decided this complicated matter needed some airing and suggested that the exercise at the end of this chapter should focus on this. Members hoped that this might lead to debate amongst those employed in working with the seriously mentally ill and perhaps encourage professionals to feel free to discuss such issues openly.

SUMMING UP

As we have seen, the LEAP group were very concerned about this case and the professional practice of those carrying out Dave's mental health assessments. Members felt that they abdicated their responsibilities and left the sufferer and his family to fend for themselves.

They were encouraged by, and full of admiration for, the skills and caring shown by the other professionals involved in the crisis – the CPNs and the police – and their determination to see this properly resolved. However, these efforts served to emphasise the apparent detachment throughout of those whose task it was to use the mental health legislation to prevent this crisis turning into a disaster.

INFORMATION

The following information is relevant to points brought up during the group's analysis and discussion which have been highlighted in the text:

(1) The part played by the police in mental health crisis situations

Families frequently report that it is the police who have eventually responded to their unanswered pleas for help, for example:

(a) an unpublished survey of 889 National Schizophrenia Fellowship members revealed that 161 sufferers obtained no help for their first episode of a serious mental illness until the police intervened (Mary Tyler 1986)

(b) a National Schizophrenia Fellowship survey carried out on behalf of the Department of Health revealed that among the 563 carers who took part, the police were the most highly rated service when it comes to caring for the mentally ill, *Provision of Community Services for Mentally Ill People and Their Carers* (1990).

(2) Factors to be taken into account at assessment

Those factors which should be considered, in addition to meeting the statutory criteria for compulsory admission under the Act, are detailed on pages 4 to 6 of the Code of Practice, Mental Health Act 1983.

(3) The killing of a sufferer in his cell by another sufferer

In November, 1994 a 30-year-old man, known to be mentally vulnerable, was remanded in custody in Chelmsford Prison for a minor public order offence. According to the *Church Times,* 14th November 1997, in an article headed 'A simple call for justice', 24 hours later he had been kicked to death by his cell-mate (known to the system as a man who suffers with a serious mental illness). The long-awaited results of an independent inquiry are not available at the time of writing.

EXERCISE

During their analysis and further discussion about the issues raised in this case study, the LEAP group focused on their concerns that when a relapse of a psychotic illness threatens, health professionals sometimes seem to be more like bystanders than paid employees of a system set up to help and support those living with a serious mental illness.

Do you feel it is possible to argue that a combination of cumbersome procedures and a legacy of ambivalent civil liberty issues have made it rather too easy for those professionals who wish to distance themselves from the wastage and suffering to do this?

CHAPTER 6

Carers and a need for caring

It seems that some sufferers survive in spite of the system rather than because of it; they survive because of the extraordinary determination of their families to tap every available resource on their behalf whenever relapse threatens. Let's take a look at the experiences of Sue's family over the past four years.

CASE STUDY

In common with most members of our society, Sue's parents had little knowledge about serious mental illness when she became ill at 22 years of age. However, after a nightmare few months of trying to get help for her, they lost no time in learning everything they could about psychosis and about the system. In answer to their questions, they were told that Sue had suffered symptoms which were typical of acute schizophrenia but the mood swings of the past few months and the manic behaviour which finally brought her the help she needed could be indicative of a manic depressive illness (MD). More importantly they noted, their daughter was responding to the medication she was prescribed and her parents were delighted to be told by the psychiatrist that she believed this would be just a 'one-off' episode. Nevertheless, they also noted the fact that that there were other young people on the ward whose parents had been given a similar prognosis but who were now having a second or third breakdown. They also picked up from these parents that their experiences told them that taking medication indefinitely was the only way to stay well with a psychotic illness.

Nevertheless, Sue's parents had every reason to gain confidence as time went on. Everything was going very well: soon after she came out of hospital Sue returned to her job and shortly afterwards she found a new boyfriend who was clearly very important to her. Around a year after she had come out of hospital, Sue came home from work and told her mother, Jan, that she didn't have to go along for any more outpatient appointments as the psychiatrist agreed she was really well now. A few days later she told her mother that she had nearly run out of medication and had thought about this and decided not to get another prescription. Jan queried this and asked her daughter to discuss it first with the GP but Sue said that wouldn't be necessary; like the psychiatrist said, she was well now.

Jan noted that no one at the GP's surgery queried the fact that Sue had not ordered her usual prescription the following month and when she had reason to see their doctor about her own health a few weeks later, she mentioned that Sue had given up on her medication. The GP didn't seem to be concerned about this and reminded the older woman how well her daughter had recovered from her breakdown. Jan felt reassured. When all was said and done, the doctor was the expert and he'd known Sue since she was a child.

However, within three weeks or so of having this conversation, Jan began to suspect that things were going wrong again although she couldn't even explain to her husband why she felt this. It took another few weeks before he could see that their daughter's behaviour was changing and this was not good news. Her moods had started 'yo-yoing' again and she was complaining about friends and colleagues at work being two-faced and talking behind her back. Very soon, her mother and father recognized that Sue was becoming paranoid about them once more, treating them with barely concealed hostility.

They decided to have a word with their daughter; they explained they were a little worried about her – she didn't seem to be her usual cheerful self – and they suggested she might go and see the GP for a check up. Sue quickly assured them that she had no intention of going anywhere near any doctors so that they could put her away again, thank you! A day or so later when Sue appeared to be quiet and calm, Jan asked her whether or not she had thought about taking her medication again for a while. Sue looked at her for a moment and got up and walked to the door, pausing only to turn round and snap at Jan, her eyes blazing with anger, 'Yes, I understand exactly why you would want me to keep taking the pills, mother'.

Jan went to see the GP and told him what was happening and he shook his head and said that Sue must come and see him herself if she needed help; he couldn't force his attentions on her. Jan couldn't believe she was hearing this again, the second time round; if she already knew that sufferers didn't seek help once they were paranoid, surely doctors were aware of it? Feeling disappointed and angry, Jan then phoned the psychiatrist only to find next day that she had left a similar message with her secretary; she would be pleased to see Sue if the young woman cared to ring herself and arrange an appointment.

From that point onwards, the family's problems escalated by the day and Jan went everywhere she could think of to try and get help for her daughter and alerted both the GP and the psychiatrist every time things deteriorated further. Having learned about her rights as the nearest relative, she even asked the local Social Services department if an ASW could come and assess her daughter. However, it turned out there wasn't time to explore this further because Sue walked out on her job and ended her relationship with her boyfriend on the same day that her mother was making this request. That night, she rushed out of the house, screaming at her parents that they wanted rid of her. She didn't return.

A few days later her parents received a card posted locally, with a picture of their home town on it, saying 'I've gone where someone really cares. I'll be all right'. The parents were distraught with worry about their vulnerable daughter. Their efforts to trace her whereabouts came to nothing; she was never spotted in their home town although a lot of people kept an eye out for her. Jan became quite seriously depressed during the months which followed, withdrawing from her friends and giving up all the interests which usually mattered to her. It was the not knowing which she and her husband found so agonizing.

Four months passed before Sue turned up on their doorstep late one night. Jan and her husband couldn't believe how dreadful she looked. She was painfully thin, with enormous staring eyes in a haggard and drawn face. There were scratches and bruises on her face and arms; she'd been in a fight, she muttered, and she'd been thrown out of the commune she'd been told about. The young woman was edgy, restless and smouldering, with her eye on the front door all the time.

Within an hour she was gone again into the darkness even as her father called out to her to come and tuck into the meal her mother had prepared. A quick search of the immediate vicinity achieved nothing. The parents looked at each other in despair – what now? They gained a little comfort from the feeling that Sue might well stay in the locality as she had sought them out and she did seem to be desperate. They could only hope they were right. Jan immediately phoned the police and the duty ASW, telling them that their daughter was ill and they felt she was at breaking point. The police took the details but the duty ASW merely told the mother to call the police again if Sue returned and rang off.

In the morning, Jan alerted the GP, the psychiatrist, the hospital where Sue had been treated previously and Social Services again. She also contacted friends, neighbours, work colleagues, everyone who knew Sue and who had been concerned when she had gone missing, asking them to look out for her. Later, an ASW turned up 'to offer support' but as she was going out of the door, she reiterated her colleague's instruction of the previous night: to ring the police if Sue turned up. As Jan opened her mouth to query this, the social worker suggested she could go further than this; why not go out and see if she could find Sue? If she was making a nuisance of herself in a public place then she should find a policeman; she added, as she hurried down the path, 'and get him to carry out a Section 136 and take Sue to a "safe place"'. When she had gone, the parents looked at each other in wonder; 'I thought social workers were meant to help in a mental health crisis, not the police', sighed the father. 'Yes', Jan wailed, 'and can you imagine going up to a policeman and telling him what to do?'

During the next 24 hours it became severely cold and a couple of inches of snow signalled the weather was not going to improve. There had been two reports that Sue had been seen and her father followed each of these up while Jan updated everyone she thought might be able to help. The following morning, her networking paid off and a friend phoned to say he had just seen Sue in a local park but she had ran off when he called her. Jan immediately alerted the police and Social Services. A police constable caught up with Sue an hour or so later, half-frozen and almost hysterical.

For some reason, it took most of the rest of the day to admit Sue to hospital and as her parents came away from seeing her settled down there mid-evening, the ASW who had admitted her told the parents that he was beginning to realize that Sue needed to be on a Section 3 instead of the 6-month Section 2 he had applied for. He had mentioned this on the ward but he advised the parents to keep on to them about converting the section. Once more the parents were astonished but they did discuss this with staff on the ward when they had the opportunity.

However, by the end of a week they realized with growing horror that the ward team, none of whom had been involved with their daughter before, had decided that Sue was not psychotic at all; they believed she was enjoying herself 'play-acting' and having everyone run around in circles after her. Now dumbfounded, they noted their daughter rushing around the ward excitedly and noisily, looking gaunt and ill, and saying completely mad things all the time she was alone with them. In despair, they asked each other how the experts could not see something was very wrong?

Once more, Jan was desperate and she persuaded an influential friend of the family who knew Sue really well to accompany them on their next visit to the hospital. This friend had no trouble at all persuading the ward staff just how paranoid Sue really was after he had finished walking in the grounds with her, listening to her detailed, insane, plans to do away with a nurse who was planning to kill her. He told them he thought it a good idea to warn them that the nurse in question might be very much at risk! He also made it clear that he considered his young friend to be completely mad at the present time. Jan noted with relief that he had succeeded where she and her husband had failed. Later, she asked her husband, 'Do you think other parents are treated this way?' He suspected they must be; 'No one has ever singled us out for special treatment, good or bad,' he sighed. 'I don't see why they should start now.'

As a result of this timely intervention, Sue was at last put on anti-psychotic drugs ten days into her 28-day section. By the time the section was due to expire, she was starting to relate well to her parents and generally showing signs of becoming her old self again. This was something which Jan and her husband had given up on again and again during recent months. They wanted to hug everyone they were so brimming with emotion and gratitude! However, they also applied themselves to practical matters and asked once more what was happening about Sue's section being converted? They were told not to worry; everything would be fine!

In the event when Sue realized her section had expired, she didn't attempt to leave the hospital but she did refuse to take her tablets. The parents learned of this a few days later when she was becoming edgy and irritable and constantly glancing round behind her. Once out in the grounds, their daughter told them that two of the patients on the ward were out to get her and she was therefore coming home where she'd be safe. When Jan talked with a doctor about this he promised to try and persuade Sue to have her medication again. He also said 'Yes, we hear you' when the father asked when the section would be renewed?

The next day, although nothing had been done about her expired section, Sue was persuaded to start taking her medication again. Two weeks later, the parents were asked to take her home; her bed was needed for an emergency admission. Her parents felt cruelly let down; not only had all the promises and reassurances come to nothing – but there had been no attempt to provide a care plan for Sue. When Jan asked what they were meant to do next she was told that Sue would be given an outpatient appointment for four weeks' time. The family was on its own once more!

When she came home, Sue showed none of the potential she had after her first breakdown. She was restless and unable to concentrate on any one thing and she was completely lacking in confidence. She continued to suffer quite excessive mood swings. When things deteriorated two weeks later to the point that they thought Sue might relapse once more, Jan phoned the hospital and insisted that something was done. Eventually, the outpatient appointment was brought forward by ten days and Sue was seen by a different psychiatrist. This in turn resulted in the young woman agreeing to take extra medication and to go back into hospital on a voluntary basis when a bed was available and three weeks later she was admitted under the supervision of this new doctor.

By the time Sue was discharged, the constant threat of relapse was fading although she still resisted taking medication and had persuaded her new psychiatrist that she should take a minimal dose. She was now allocated a CPN and put under the care of a local mental health team. For the first time in over a year her parents felt able to relax a little and even found that sometimes they could now sleep the night through. As they gradually adjusted to the idea that they didn't have to fight every inch of the way to protect their daughter from further damage, friends reported that they could see the years dropping off them. However, as Jan now puts it, 'this new sense of security was all rather naive as it turned out, but it was good at the time'.

Two years later Sue remains vulnerable and unable to work but she has moved into a flat near to her parents home. She frequently visits them and seeks their help whenever she feels particularly vulnerable. The young woman now has some insight into her illness but she is still on a minimal dose of medication so she tends to become very ill in a matter of hours and without any real warning. Furthermore, and in common with a lot of sufferers, such times for Sue seem to occur at any time other than nine to five on an ordinary weekday. Twice in the past six months when her daughter has been on the point of relapse, Jan has ended up running around sorting things out for her because the CPN and other members of the mental health team are not available at night time or weekends or public holidays.

Again and again, Jan has wondered what happens to sufferers who have no family to support them and fight for their interests? 'How can community care work on a part-time basis?' she asks. Jan knows that until things are very different she and her husband can't have the two things they most crave and which many of us take for granted; some peace and some time to themselves. They have found out the hard way that Sue becomes even more vulnerable if she knows her parents aren't available for her.

Jan believes that nothing will change until the system operates on a full-time basis or until professionals start to liaise with and work in partnership with carers, recognizing that their needs have to be taken into account if they are to continue to 'provide the majority of care to the mentally ill' (1).

COMMENT

This case study demonstrates rather well why some families find themselves fighting continuously for the survival of a relative with a psychotic illness. Whatever their own coping mechanisms may be, they become totally dependent on professionals to rescue them from a constant threat of disaster. The help they need may be refused, as when Sue was showing the early signs of relapse when she came off medication, or it may not be available because crisis situations tend to occur outside normal working hours. The only continuity in care may be that provided by families, and they in turn find themselves having to relate to a succession of different professionals. Meanwhile, between emergencies, the system is happy to leave the carers to get on with it.

Like Jan and her husband, most do this at considerable cost to their own quality of life while all the time dreading the next time disaster threatens.

Perhaps it might be worthwhile to pause for a moment and read through the case study again imagining that you are one of Sue's parents. Having achieved that, in what ways do you think you might like to change or improve the service you have received?

GROUP'S ANALYSIS OF THE CASE STUDY

Members were exasperated by the system's apparent inability to get a grip on this young woman's illness before it could destroy so much of this young woman's potential to live a normal lifestyle. As the case study has laid emphasis on the family's experience of trying to obtain effective help for the sufferer, the group decided to focus their analysis on this aspect of living with a serious mental illness.

Getting into the System

They noted that Jan and her husband had 'a nightmare few months' of trying to get their daughter into the system when she first became ill and that while this is not an uncommon experience (2), it had a profound effect on them. They made sure they learned as much as they could about psychotic illness and the system in the hope they would avoid any more of the same.

Early signs of relapse

The group found it very sad that after a year of keeping so well, Sue's doctors declined to 'stop the rot' when she started to deteriorate after coming off her medication. 'This is something which seems to come up again and again', grumbled a carer 'with doctors refusing to intervene when their patient starts to deteriorate instead of using the law as was intended "in the interests of her health". It makes me so cross!' (3)

'Yes', agreed a survivor, 'doctors know that only a minority of sufferers will have just one episode of illness and the rest will remain vulnerable (4) so why do they just go away and stick their heads in the sand when the inevitable happens?' The group wondered if the first psychiatrist warned Sue that she might remain vulnerable and might find she needed to take medication later or whether she just assured her she was well now and that was that? They knew this important subject was often avoided completely and a survivor felt this was quite unacceptable; 'like I've said before,' she reminded everyone, 'there's no way that professionals should turn their back on a sufferer for some while after they've stopped taking their medication, like they did with me. They're abdicating their responsibilities in my opinion'.

Other members agreed with this and were not at all impressed with the reaction of either of Sue's doctors when her mother sought their help. 'Once again, why on earth didn't the GP arrange for a domicillary visit by a psychiatrist. Don't these doctors realize that's what this provision is for?' asked another survivor(5).

Either way, the group had no doubt that it was downhill all the way from the point that the GP and psychiatrist turned their backs on their patient.

Gone missing

The group went on to discuss the effect that Sue's disappearance had on her parents and, in particular, the mother, who seemed to have become depressed. 'And who could wonder at that?' asked a carer, 'when her daughter was already very vulnerable!'

The group knew of several cases where a carer had even ended up in hospital with severe depression after the system failed to protect their vulnerable relative. 'It's madness, really, isn't it?' a carer commented, 'they end up with two patients instead of one and with nothing at all resolved'. 'Yes, like in Kim's case (see Chapter 2) – prolonged tension and worry just wore the mother down, so sometimes they not only end up with two patients, but they lose a full-time carer as well!', someone pointed out.

Other members commented on cases they knew about where carers had actually moved away – had to disappear, in fact – because the system failed again and again to support them at times of crisis. This seemed to them to be a damning indictment on the services provided for those trying to cope with a serious mental illness.

Trying to get back into the system

Members next looked at the reaction of the two ASWs who seemed determined to persuade these parents to call the police if their daughter turned up. They assumed that reports of Sue's 'smouldering anger' and 'unkempt appearance' had for some reason alerted them to a possibility of violence; 'but that's what psychosis is all about!' protested a carer, 'Unpredictability is what it's all about!'

'Yes', said a survivor thoughtfully, 'it seems to me that these social workers are afraid of violence – aren't we all? But leaving it to the police would involve the criminal law and that's just not acceptable.' 'No, that's right. We're back with the phenomenon we discussed in Dave's case, aren't we?', agreed another survivor. 'It seems that some ASWs just pass the buck, now, instead of seeking police back-up when they need it: "police assistance" they call it in the Code of Practice which seems very different to telling families to go away and get on with it themselves!' (6). 'And anyway' a carer pointed out 'Social Services have a duty to arrange a mental health assessment if the nearest relative requests this' (7).

'But, what about the second ASW telling the mother to go and look for her daughter and then find a policeman and tell him to do a Section 136?' grinned a survivor. The group felt this was a really new development and one which raised all sorts of hilarious prospects. When the laughter died down, a carer pointed out, 'but it's very worrying that these ASWs should be so anxious to pass the buck, or anyway to avoid meeting the sufferer unless the police were already involved, isn't it?' Indeed, members could quite imagine why this mother might be starting to wonder what happened to sufferers who didn't have families to fight for their interests.

The wrong section?

LEAP group members were at a loss to understand why the third ASW had applied for a different section to the one he later felt would be the right one. 'There's little doubt the social worker had Sue's best interests at heart but he really did let her down badly, didn't he?' a carer pointed out. 'Yes, these parents were going to have trouble persuading the ward team that their daughter was ill, let alone persuading them to accept advice on how the law should be used!', another carer concluded grimly.

Given that the ASW did leave this problem with the parents, members discussed what hospital doctors could have done about converting the section. They concluded that once the ward team realized belatedly that Sue needed treatment then her Section 2 should have been converted to a Section 3. Indeed, a glance at the Code of Practice should confirm that the law makes provision for this (8).

Someone pointed out that as the ward team had not taken this step, they should certainly have done something about protecting Sue when her 28-day section expired; everyone agreed it was clear she was not well at this time and that the paranoia was scarcely under control. Yes, there seemed to be no doubt that this was a second opportunity to use the law to protect their patient 'if the will had been there to do this', as one member put it.

Not listening to the family

At this point, members came back to the matter of the ward team not recognizing that Sue was ill. One carer was amazed at this, 'I don't understand this at all!', she told the group, 'What is all their training for if they don't recognize when someone is psychotic?'

Other members weren't quite so surprised and two survivors in the group thought this could happen quite frequently if their own experience was anything to go by. 'But it's a case of not listening to, or giving credibility to, those closest to the sufferer, isn't it?' one of them pointed out. Yes, there seemed to be no doubt about that and she continued, 'if they'd asked these parents what their daughter was usually like or had bothered to read her notes, they would have realized Sue was not the excitable, attention-seeking personality they took her to be'.

'I have to say that this is the point in this case study which makes me really angry', complained a carer whose own son went missing for a time when he was ill. 'How could these professionals treat these parents as being of no importance or concern after what they had been through during the past months? To me, this is arrogant as well as uncaring!'

'Yes, and isn't it interesting that this mother had to sort the professionals out and find someone whom they would listen to?'

observed a second carer. 'It seems to me that she has had to organize every aspect of her daughter's care from start to finish of this case!' This last comment certainly seemed to reflect the feelings of the group.

Betrayal?

Members were very sad that the poor practice they had already commented on was finally compounded by the team's reaction to a shortage of beds. 'Sue was not only sent home before she had a chance to recover from her long illness, she was not provided with any adequate arrangements for her immediate needs' a survivor protested, 'let alone with a care plan.'

The group felt this was a betrayal for these parents. 'I think this ward team was very unprofessional from start to finish. They didn't have the skills to recognize the patient was ill and they didn't have the humility to recognize her parents might have a little more expertize on this subject than them!' exclaimed a survivor. 'Yes, and they didn't know about, or care about – we don't know which – using the law properly either', a carer agreed.

Breakthrough and high hopes

The LEAP group members were relieved and encouraged to learn about the next stage of Sue's experiences with the system. They were impressed that she was offered another opportunity to go into hospital and that she was persuaded to go into hospital of her own accord. 'This saved any more unnecessary trauma for her and the family, didn't it?', a delighted survivor said.

The group was equally impressed that this time Sue went on to have a properly planned discharge with arrangements being made for her to come under the care of a local mental health team as well as having a CPN to keep an eye on her. Several members felt it was a shame that Sue's new psychiatrist had not been able to use this positive experience of Sue's to persuade her to have enough medication to give her proper protection. As one survivor put it, 'the trouble with taking too low a dose is that you never feel really secure – too often there's shadowy symptoms hovering in the background – well that's what I found anyway'. Another survivor wondered if any of Sue's doctors had taken the trouble to find out why she so disliked taking her medication, 'She might have had undesirable side effects, of course, but it didn't sound this way when she just upped and got on with her life after her first breakdown', she added. Others in the group felt it sad that this was still an unresolved issue.

Nevertheless, things seemed to be improving for Sue and her family at last and a carer remarked that 'This admission seems to have been a very different experience to the previous one and it resulted in these parents having some peace of mind for the first time in a long while'. Several members of the group could identify very well with how that might feel.

The reality

Members noted that two years later Sue had now taken the considerable step of moving out of her parents' home while keeping close contact with them. So far so good, they felt, but everything seemed to be very precarious nonetheless. 'Increasingly, Sue's survival seems to rely on her parents being there to intervene each time she's in trouble', a carer observed 'and, meanwhile, there's little time and opportunity for them to have a life of their own, more's the pity'.

'Well, can you wonder at it?', asked another carer. 'It stands to reason that families are going to provide the real community care when the services only operate fully during office working hours!'

'And it isn't as if service providers admit this – they don't!' a survivor commented, 'so somehow or other they take over whenever they're available and leave families to cope with all the problems that occur in between – well, that's how it seems to me, anyway!'

'That's right; I don't think its going to work until professionals work in partnership with carers like Jan says', agreed a carer, 'and then they'd have to work out how sufferers and carers can get immediate help when they're not available!'

'Yes, that's more important to my mind than their being there all the time' someone agreed, 'particularly as that's not ever going to happen in my opinion!'

'Meanwhile', a survivor pointed out, 'the psychiatrist supervising Sue has agreed that she needn't take enough medication to protect her from these sudden near-relapses she's now prone to – but it's the parents who are the fall guys, isn't it?'

Other members felt this was indeed how it seemed to be and that this contract between Sue and her doctor only worked because Sue's parents intervened on her behalf when the professionals weren't available. 'And they can't afford not to respond to their daughter's cries for help because they are the ones who will end up picking up the pieces if things go wrong; I know, I've been there!' a carer exclaimed.

Members felt that this just about summed up the position which these parents have found themselves in after four years of tireless effort to look after their daughter's interests. They felt this analysis had come round full circle; things could have turned out very differently for this sufferer and those who love her if professionals had worked in partnership with those who knew her best and who provided the only continuity of care throughout her illness; her parents.

THE WIDER PERSPECTIVE

The LEAP group felt that this case study clearly demonstrated the reality of life for those closest to someone with a serious mental illness unless this is properly controlled from the outset. They decided to explore further how the needs of these families are commonly overlooked.

A need for respect

There was a strong feeling amongst members that Sue's nearest relative, her mother, was shown little, if any, respect by the professionals concerned with her daughter and they argued that this was one of the most common failings in the present system. Members pointed out that carers are only there because they do care and because they are close to the sufferer. 'So it stands to reason that they usually know more about that individual than any of the professionals who pass through their life, doesn't it?' commented a survivor, 'What is more', she went on, 'my nearest relative is also the person I choose to spend my life with and who knows what I want out of that life – so there's an awful lot of expertise about me there!'

This was how other members saw it too. There was a strong feeling in the group that doctors and other professionals often fail to protect sufferers properly because they underrate the resources that those nearest to them have to offer. 'More's the pity', grumbled a carer 'when you think how little continuity of care there is now. Look at what happened to Sue when no one on the ward knew her; they just jumped to conclusions instead of referring to and listening to the parents'.

'And there's more to this than just being very close to the sufferer, you know. You can't live with serious mental illness for very long without becoming quite an expert on the illness and how it affects the sufferer', a carer claimed, ' but no one seems to want to know about that either!'

'That's right', agreed a survivor, 'I often seek my family's opinion on my illness. I don't promise I'll take notice of it every time but I find it's usually worth asking!'

'I guess what we're talking about', responded a carer, 'is being respected by professionals as someone not only having to cope with living with a serious mental illness whether we like it or not but also being left to make a reasonable job of finding out how best to do this'.

'Yes, that's it, exactly!' another carer agreed emphatically, 'I'd appreciate some respect because I have worked hard at it and I do know this has helped. I'm quite shocked sometimes at how little some professionals seem to know about this type of illness'.

'I think we're back to Jan's "working in partnership" with professionals and I would certainly appreciate it if the professionals who are involved with my son would liaise with me more now he's living away from home. The CPN who's meant to be visiting him weekly said he was too busy to let me know that my son wouldn't let him in his flat for weeks and weeks. So I then find myself picking up the pieces when he relapses with no prior warning'. This group member has seen a stream of professionals come and go without any one of them taking note of her very real expertize and caring skills.

Other members agreed this was not about the CPN not having the time to make a very important phone call (perhaps during the time originally allocated to her son each week?) but a sad example of a professional underrating the person whom the system calls 'the carer'; the same person who will always be expected to 'pick up the pieces' as this mother put it.

The group then went on to discuss the apparent inability of some professionals to identify in any way with what carers have to go through at times of crisis.

A need for understanding

A carer started this discussion by saying that in the 16 years since she had become a carer she had felt again and again that most professionals had no idea at all what it might be like to be in her position. 'As some of you know' she added, 'my relative's psychosis comes out of nowhere in a matter of hours, rather like Sue's, but worse. After a nightmare couple of hours recently I managed to get to the phone and ring the GP just before his evening surgery started only to have him reply "If you wanted a home visit, why didn't you phone first thing this morning?"' She looked round at us for a moment and took a deep breath; 'I wanted to scream at him "you don't know you're alive do you?". Instead, I just go on hoping that that one day they'll understand just what it means to be out there on your own with someone who has just become raging psychotic'.

'Let alone understanding just how much time and effort you put into keeping things on an even keel and not making demands on the service the rest of the time!' a member who is a friend of this family observed with deep feeling.

'Yes, that's right', she nodded gratefully, 'and the way it feels when my relative sometimes has to be admitted to hospital and I hate myself because its all happened again. No one seems to care. Everyone talks about trauma counselling these days but no one even offers me a kind word. Do they still blame us families for the illness, do you think?'

'I'm not sure about that, but I think it's possible,' a survivor responded. 'Something shocked me recently. A girl at work was telling me about the worst moment of her life: she was 22 at the time and her live-in boyfriend became ill. It was a first episode of MD apparently, and he had to be admitted to hospital. She said she'd never forget it, nor would she forget the ASW, a woman, who turned round and snapped at her "what are *you* crying for?" as she went out of the door'.

'Yes', sighed a carer 'perhaps that says it all. Can anyone imagine a so-called caring professional feeling anything other than sympathy, if not pity, for this young woman at a time like that, unless they took the attitude that it was her fault anyway and that she was having her boyfriend put away because he was a nuisance?' 'Oh, dear', a survivor exclaimed, 'that poor girl needed a hug and being told that this wasn't necessarily the end of everything that mattered to her. How sad!'

'This is a very telling story, isn't it?', a carer observed, 'I really do think that every professional training course should include a section on professional attitudes towards carers and that this young woman's experience could well feature in this'. Members felt that this brief story went a long way to explaining why carers often come to feel like victims when they seek help from the system (see Chapter 2 for an earlier discussion on this).

A need for caring

Returning to the earlier comment that this young woman needed a hug after watching her boyfriend being forcibly taken to hospital, the LEAP group members paused for a moment to consider just what else carers need after they have been through a psychotic crisis and a loved one has finally been sectioned.

'No one who has not experienced it could ever imagine in their wildest dreams just what this feels like', a mother said quietly. 'Even the professionals, most of them anyway, who see it happen again and again show no recognition of what it feels like to see your own son being forcibly taken to hospital'.

The words trauma and traumatized came up again and again and so did the memories of feelings of inadequacy, of guilt, and of frustration, despite the relief of having the crisis resolved. Members talked about fear too; fear that it could, or, in some cases, most certainly would, happen again.

Several members talked of an incident at a meeting of carers they had attended when an ASW had said that she always likes to return to a family the day after she has sectioned a sufferer to give them a chance to talk it through and to make sure they're coping with what has happened. She seemed shocked when she was told that none of the seven carers present whose relatives had been sectioned one or more times had ever had such an experience at any time. These carers would certainly have appreciated such a service; they were even touched to feel that this social worker had seen a need for this. One described this to us now as 'actually having someone come round to help pick up the pieces – and that's the only way you could describe me and my family at this point'. 'Yes', another agreed with her, 'just to know someone cares; that's enough to be going on with, isn't it?'

The group finished their discussion at this point, having, perhaps, made it very clear that there was ample room for improvement in the service provided to those individuals who were in fact just expected to keep on caring, whatever.

SUMMING UP

In this chapter, the LEAP group members have looked at how the mishandling of a serious mental illness can affect the lives of a whole family. They found an absence of any serious attempt by the professionals who have passed through Sue's life to liaise with her parents or to even heed what they might have to say about their daughter and her illness. They also noted that, despite her parents' vigorous efforts, the law was not used properly to protect their daughter from unnecessary damage.

Finally, the group looked at some of the ways that carers could be used as a valued resource as well as cared for in their own right. They felt that both issues had to be a real priority, particularly now that these are the individuals who increasingly provide the only continuity of care for many sufferers.

INFORMATION

The following information is relevant to points brought up during this chapter which have been highlighted in the text:

(1) Carers as major providers of community care

Health of the Nation 'Building Bridges' states, under the heading Care Programme Approach:

> 'Carers often provide the majority of care to mentally ill people. Their contribution to meeting users' needs should be explicitly recognized in the Care Plan. Help from the Mental Health Services would include meeting the carers' needs for support, periods of respite care and 24-hour access to an emergency mental health service.' (See Department of Health, 1996 *Health of the Nation* 'Building Bridges', London: HMSO.)

(2) Delays and difficulties in getting into the system

In their study of 462 first episodes of schizophrenia, E. C. Johnstone and her colleagues found that the interval between onset of illness and admission varied widely, but was often more than one year and associated with severe behavioural disturbance and family difficulty in arranging appropriate care. These workers concluded that their findings 'allowed no interpretation other than that appropriate services were not available to these people when they were required' (Johnstone, E. C. *et al* (1986) The Northwick Park Study of First Episodes of Schizophrenia, Part I: 'Presentation of the Illness and Problems Relating to Admission', *British Journal of Psychiatry, 148,* 115–120).

(3) Sectioning in the interests of the patient's health

The Code of Practice of the Mental Health Act 1983 makes it clear that the Act allows for the sectioning of a patient 'in the interests of his health' – see the Foreword, last paragraph, on p. iii and also that this point is reiterated in paragraph 2.6 of the Code of Practice.

(4) A questionable 'statistic'?

Bleuler's finding that 'at least 25 per cent of all schizophrenics recover entirely (after one breakdown) and remain recovered for good' has been widely accepted and quoted (see Bleuler M., 'The long-term course of schizophrenic psychoses' in Wynne, Cromwell and Matthysse (eds) *The Nature of Schizophrenia,* 1978, New York: Wiley, pp. 631–6).

However, an interesting aspect of Bleuler's findings is less well known; his criteria for 'recovery' apparently allow for the persistence of symptoms such as delusions and perceptual disturbance. It would seem there is a good case for believing that the vast majority of those having a first episode of this type of illness would be well advised to assume they might be vulnerable to, at best, further symptoms of psychosis and, at worst, further episodes of the illness.

(5) Domicillary consultations – an underused resource?

In their study of 462 first episodes of schizophrenia, E. C. Johnstone and her colleagues found that 'in particular, knowledge of the availability of domicillary consultations for patients who refused to visit doctors or hospitals was not widespread' (Johnstone, E.C. *et al* (1986) The Northwick Park Study of First Episodes of Schizophrenia, Part 1: 'Presentation of the Illness and Problems Relating to Admission', *British Journal of Psychiatry, 148*, 115-120)

LEAP group members have noted several cases where a domicillary visit by a psychiatrist might well have prevented a threatened crisis when families have sought help from their GP.

(6) To call the police?

As we noted in Chapter 5, there seems to be an increasing incidence of families known to the LEAP group being told by ASWs to call the police. However, Paragraph 2.4 the *Code of Practice* states that:

> 'Everyone involved in assessment should be aware of the need to provide mutual support, especially where there is a risk of the patient causing serious physical harm (including, where necessary, the need to call for police assistance and how to use that assistance to minimise the risk of violence)' (see p. 3, Paragraph 2.4)

Neither this statement nor the duty conferred on Social Services departments to arrange a mental health assessment for a sufferer if the nearest relative requests this (see reference (7) below) seems to imply that families should be left to ring the police rather than the duty ASW if there is any risk of violence.

(7) The nearest relative's request for a mental health assessment

If the nearest relative requests a mental health assessment then Section 13.4 of the Mental Health Act 1983 puts a duty on the local Social Services department to arrange for an ASW to assess with a view to deciding whether or not to make an application for the sufferer's admission to hospital.

(8) When Section 2 is not appropriate

Indicators for using Section 3 are listed under the heading *Section 3 pointers* of the *Code of Practice*. Paragraph 5.3c would appear to be particularly relevant to the proposed conversion discussed several times in this chapter (see p. 22).

EXERCISE

In the third and present chapters in this book, the LEAP group has discussed the idea that carers can seem to be victims of mental health service provision. They have also discussed the fact that families are often the major providers of community care. There seems to be an argument here for supposing that many of those who are having to make the concept of 'care in the community' viable nevertheless have cause to feel they are abused by the system which is meant to be providing this.

What evidence can you find in this chapter which supports such an argument?

CHAPTER 7

A reluctance to use the law?

At the time of writing there is still little sign that the system can respond immediately to calls for help when relapse threatens and while sufferers are still aware enough to accept help. Until such time as everyone concerned realizes that this *critical period* provides the most painless and cost-effective answer to treating serious mental illness in the community, then families have no choice but to rely on professionals to be pro-active and *use the law* sooner rather than later. However, there are health professionals who show a pronounced reluctance to use the law and many more seem to be unaware of the provision it makes for protecting sufferers from unnecessary damage. The following brief case studies demonstrate in their different ways how we seem to be caught up in a 'no win' and 'no winners' approach to handling relapse situations.

CASE STUDY

Clive, a quiet and sensitive young man of 23 years, became ill overnight. Suddenly, with no warning of any sort, he turned on his mother and held her captive for several hours, punching her and holding her down when she tried to leave the room. This was just the start of this terrifying and uncharacteristic behaviour; every so often, and with no warning, Clive would turn on his mother again and she sometimes fled her own home for days at a time. Despite these horrific experiences, she could not get anyone to take her son's sudden and dramatic change of personality seriously once the family GP had referred him onto the psychiatric services.

In one of his quieter moods, Clive told his mother he thought he was going mad. It seemed that a psychiatrist he had seen several times at the local hospital did not share this viewpoint and when Clive decided not to attend one of his outpatient appointments his mother wrote to the doctor asking for his help, explaining just how bad things were becoming. He wrote back telling her that as Clive didn't seem to want his help there was nothing he could do.

However, Clive did seek this psychiatrist's help 15 months later and told the older man that he wanted to be detained in hospital because if he was free to leave he knew he wouldn't stay there. The psychiatrist responded by agreeing to admit him to hospital, but on a voluntary basis. The next day Clive discharged himself. This happened twice more in the following weeks and then he disappeared for several days. By this time, other members of his family understood just how ill he was and regularly contacted the hospital team to express their anxiety.

On his return to his mother's home, dishevelled, excited and gaunt-looking, Clive went straight to his GP's surgery and asked him to lock him up somewhere as he was sure he'd do someone an injury the way he felt. During the previous week, Clive had been diagnosed as having a schizophrenic illness and had just been prescribed antipsychotic medication. The doctor asked the hospital to arrange a bed for his patient and Clive was admitted later that day, again on a voluntary basis, despite his mother's pleas that he should be detained under the Mental Health Act as he had been requesting.

Clive didn't discharge himself this time; instead, as he was free to come and go, he went home most days to his mother who was almost beside herself with worry. One night he attempted suicide by taking an overdose of the tranquillizers she had been prescribed. Two evenings later he walked onto the railway line in front of an approaching train.

By the time appropriate treatment was made available to this young man, he was not able to take advantage of it. As far as his family were concerned, Clive died because he couldn't persuade anyone to listen to him when he at last understood how he could be helped.

CASE STUDY

Malcolm's case study was featured in Chapter 5 of *Getting into the System* (the first book in this series). Here we shall look at just that part of his story in which missed opportunities to use the law delayed his obtaining a diagnosis, treatment and care for his illness by at least another two years.

Malcolm, at 17 years, had been very sick for 12 months when his mother told their GP that she could not cope much longer. Malcolm was becoming increasingly threatening. The GP said she could do nothing as he was refusing to accept help; Malcolm had originally agreed to go into an adolescent unit for assessment but since his discharge from there, with no diagnosis nor medication, he had refused to keep his outpatient appointments or to see the GP at her surgery. He was now too sick to understand that he needed help.

One night, three months after her visit to the GP and when her husband was working late, Malcolm threatened his mother, holding a bread knife to her throat. His young brothers (both of primary school age) watched in horror, screaming with fear. Later that night, Malcolm was eventually persuaded by an ASW and a psychiatrist to go into hospital on a voluntary basis. He stayed there for nine days, when he discharged himself.

When the distraught parents pleaded for the hospital to do something, a doctor told them that Malcolm was 'not sectionable' after having the benefit of sanctuary and medication, but they would keep a bed for him.

The young man quickly deteriorated again and matters went from bad to worse, with school teachers expressing concern about the welfare and progress of the two younger boys and with health professionals suddenly talking about Malcolm's 'bad behaviour' rather than illness. In fact, they asked the parents why they were prepared to put up with such behaviour? When he first became ill, the parents had been given to understand that they were to blame for Malcolm's problems; now , they gathered, it seemed that it was all his own fault and illness was no longer mentioned.

A couple of months later, when his mother tried to persuade Malcolm to get out of bed for an outpatient appointment she had arranged for him, he attacked her. In tears she went to the GP with her blackened eye, begging for help. The GP sympathized but said 'you don't have to put up with this sort of behaviour you know!' At this point, the parents had no choice but to find accommodation for Malcolm with the help of a social worker who had been suggesting this for some weeks.

During the next 18 months, his now seriously depressed mother frequently trekked the streets with her son searching for new accommodation as one outraged landlady after another turned this troubled boy out. Eventually, Malcolm was found by the police trying to set fire to his latest digs. He was then sectioned and received treatment and care for his long-standing schizophrenic illness. Some years later, he still requires 24-hour care.

CASE STUDY

Jean and Kevin married in their early twenties, having known each other since childhood. Things started going wrong 18 months later after Kevin took up a demanding job in a local branch of a big engineering firm. Despite the fact that he seemed to enjoy this, he talked incessantly about his work and fretted about everything concerned with it. Up at all hours of the night, he made a drama out of everything and was becoming hostile and verbally abusive to Jean. She persuaded him to see his GP but the tranquillizers prescribed for him didn't help. After several nights without sleep, things rapidly worsened and Kevin finally became so manic during a visit from his parents that they rang the GP. Two ASWs and a local GP arranged an emergency admission to hospital.

The couple were told that the stress of his work had caused the breakdown. Jean gave Kevin all the support she could when he was made redundant. He eventually found another job and things settled down again for about two years until, suddenly, Jean realized it was all happening again. Kevin's behaviour gradually escalated into mania and he was compulsorily admitted to hospital once more. This time, the couple were told that he was suffering with manic depression (MD) and he was put on lithium.

After this episode, Kevin was once more made redundant. This time, he attended a day centre until he was offered a job which involved driving. A few months later he was sacked from this because he had not revealed his medical history or the fact that he was on medication. The stress of this affected Kevin's mental health but he managed to keep relatively well on a maintenance dose of lithium for a further two years during which time the couple's relationship resumed a normal footing. Because Kevin seemed completely well again, his psychiatrist agreed that he could come off his medication.

Two weeks after he stopped taking the medication, Jean realized things were going wrong again and Kevin told her that his mind was racing. He agreed with Jean that they should try to get an emergency appointment with his psychiatrist. However, they had to wait a month for this. They held out as best they could but things worsened and Kevin started talking about wanting a legal separation from his wife. When they finally saw the psychiatrist, Jean was devastated to be told by him that there was nothing wrong with Kevin at that time so she would have to accept that he wanted a legal separation.

Knowing that her family and neighbours realized that Kevin hadn't been right for several weeks, Jean asked the local GPs for their help, only to be told that Kevin would have to come and see them himself. He was now past seeking help and he became increasingly paranoid about Jean and was so verbally threatening one evening that she moved out, back to her parents' home, after a local GP had refused to come out to 'a marital dispute'.

A week later, increasingly worried about his welfare, Jean rang Kevin's day centre but was told he seemed to have improved and per-haps she should just get on with her own life? Not long after this, Kevin rang his wife at work one morning, begging her to come home at once. Jean got there to find a GP and the psychiatrist with her hus-band and his exhausted father who was now taking the brunt of his son's verbal abuse and demands.

Kevin was admitted to hospital on section later that day and it was no consolation to Jean to learn that the psychiatrist told her parents-in-law that she had seen the early warning signs and had been right all along. This time, Kevin was allowed to leave hospital before he was well again and he immediately started working towards getting the separation from Jean. In the end, she felt she had no choice but to sign the agreement, hoping that if she did this and continued living in her parents' home then Kevin would realize she was not to blame for his problems. Meanwhile, she kept in touch with her husband and always responded when he contacted her.

When Kevin later moved out of the matrimonial home, he was shortly admitted to hospital again, this time severely ill. As he was re-covering from this episode, he told his wife that he needed her and she wasn't to blame for his illness; for a while they enjoyed a happy truce and became close friends again. Because delusional ideas were now becoming a real feature of his illness, Kevin's medication had been adjusted to allow for this. It suited him well but he slept too much, so the dose was later cut down by half. Soon after this, Kevin distanced himself from Jean and before long told his wife he didn't want to go on seeing her.

One year later, frustrated with trying to come to terms with his illness, Kevin still keeps in touch with Jean and often leaves messages on her answer-phone. He also regularly demands they should get a divorce and she resists letting him make this important decision while he is still so unwell. Although he now accepts he has MD and realizes it was not Jean who was making him ill, he is still reluctant to take the medication he needs to control his mood swings on a regular basis.

Meanwhile, Jean draws strength from the friendship and support she gets from the Manic Depression Fellowship (MDF) and from friends and family. She also continues to learn all she can about serious mental illness and hopes in time Kevin will be able to manage his MD.

CASE STUDY

Kay's story was featured in Chapter 6 of *Getting into the System*. A sufferer who became ill as a child, life was a nightmare for her and for her parents throughout her teens. Here we shall look at what happened when crisis threatened after she had been relatively well for three years.

Kay was diagnosed schizophrenic when she was finally referred to the adult mental health services. Treatment was only partially effective and she continued to be hostile and unhappy. Eventually, she was tried on a new anti-psychotic drug and this had a dramatic effect, and much of her frustration and delusional thinking abated. She gradually settled down into a relatively normal lifestyle. Although now quite socially inept, she was well liked at a local day centre and even chose to join a support group there and attended this regularly. She was now well supported by the system, seeing a CPN on a weekly basis and her psychiatrist frequently too. Much to her parents' pleasure, she was now relating very well to her family instead of blaming them for her problems as she had throughout her teens.

This happy phase lasted for three years, at the end of which Kay suddenly announced that she was going to gradually come off all her medication. Staff at the centre tried to get to the bottom of this but all she would say was that she had to come off her medication and must do this gradually. They, and some of her fellow clients, tried to talk Kay out of the idea but could not get through to her. Staff immediately alerted Kay's psychiatrist and her CPN, pointing out that the young woman seemed to be giving everyone plenty of opportunity to change her mind. Perhaps she hoped someone would intervene?

Later on, when she was deteriorating in front of their eyes and becoming hostile and destructive at home again, the parents pleaded with the psychiatrist to do something but they were told nothing could be done; Kay didn't want to take her medication and that was her right. Meanwhile, she continued to attend the day centre, where she behaved reasonably well but spent hours talking in an agitated monologue about her increasingly mad thoughts and her smouldering anger about all sorts of things. Centre staff reported this dramatic change in their client.

Family life once more turned into a nightmare with Kay frequently falling foul of the law as well as making life at home a nightmare. At last, over two years after she came off the medication which had helped her so much, Kay was sectioned and eventually put back on it. Sadly, it no longer controls her illness and she continues to be the cause of considerable concern.

CASE STUDY

Not long after she left school, Debbie started to become a recluse. Except for going out to her job as a bank clerk whenever she could cope with this, she locked herself in her widowed mother's bungalow.

Gradually, Debbie developed all sorts of obsessional habits; showering for hours on end and washing her hands until they were sore, and she became hostile and verbally violent towards her mother. After months of this, she confided, 'I'm scared; I'm losing it, Mum' and confirmed that she felt 'unsafe' and 'violent'. Her mother persuaded Debbie to go and see their GP, a senior in a local practice, and eventually she agreed. He gave the young woman some tablets and nothing changed.

Gradually things worsened, with Debbie becoming distraught and excited, throwing food, smashing crockery; even pulling the telephone off the wall. Her mother went to see the GP herself this time but was told 'Sorry, I can't do anything about this unless Debbie

comes and asks for help'. Weeks later, with the young woman's behaviour becoming more and more threatening, the mother went back
and was given the same message by another doctor who, while seeming sympathetic and concerned, suggested she really should ring the
police if the violent behaviour worsened.

Meanwhile, the mayhem at home was escalating every night. Debbie's mother was now becoming quite scared and she was finding she
could only sleep if she locked her bedroom door. At this time she
started to keep a suitcase packed and a key on the window-sill so that
she could escape from her home at night if necessary. Her daughter
was frequently hysterical, ranting and raving for hours on end about
everyone being after her – there were even helicopters hovering above
the home watching her – and every so often she would explode and
turn on her mother again.

This heightened terror went on for several more months, during
which time the mother rang the GPs each time a crisis occurred. They
continued to do nothing and this was the case too with the local Social Services department and the local CPN team. Because she had
gradually become sure that her daughter must be seriously ill, the
mother got in touch with the National Schizophrenia Fellowship
(NSF) and met with the local carers' group; she said later 'they were
the only ones who believed what I was saying; they gave me confidence in myself'. They also made sure she understood her rights and
persuaded her to go back to the agencies who were ignoring her
plight to insist they listen; but still to no avail.

However, her newly restored confidence inspired this mother to
find a way of obtaining undeniable evidence of the nightmare she and
her daughter were living through. She bought a small tape-recorder
and half-a-dozen tapes. Sickened with fear, and taking advantage of
the half-light of the next few early autumn evenings, she tucked this
under her arm and 'threw the switch' again and again. A few days
later, she took five partially used tapes to Social Services and de-
manded a mental health assessment for her daughter. Without listening to the tapes but clearly impressed by this mother's determination,
the duty ASW promised a mental health assessment would be arranged for the next day. However, she rang later; there was a hiccup as
Debbie's GP felt a mental health assessment would be premature. The
ASW would now get in touch with a psychiatrist who 'serviced' Debbie's area and ask his advice.

That evening, the ASW and the psychiatrist she had mentioned arrived at the home, together with a GP from the local surgery. Debbie rushed out of the bungalow. Her mother played a little of the first tape to her visitors. Later that evening, Debbie was admitted to hospital on a Section 2 under the supervision of the same psychiatrist. He told the mother that he had not come across a patient who was more seriously ill than her daughter. It took many months before she was well enough to return home. Two years later, Debbie's mother is delighted to see her daughter at peace and even starting to enjoy a relatively normal, albeit sheltered, lifestyle. However, like many other parents in a similar situation, she remains 'very frightened' for her daughter's future.

COMMENT

Perhaps the most worrying feature in four of these five cases is that professionals did not take advantage of opportunities presented by sufferers who still had enough insight to accept help. When this critical period had passed, professionals then declined to use the law to prevent the otherwise inevitable crisis.

It might be an interesting exercise at this point to read through each case study again and determine (a) at which point, if any, you believe professionals might have been able to resolve a threatened crisis with the co-operation of the sufferer and (b) the first point at which you believe the law could have been used to stop the rot really setting in.

THE GROUP'S ANALYSIS OF THESE CASE STUDIES

The group decided to look at each of these cases in turn before considering the features they have in common with each other and, where appropriate, with other cases in this book.

Clive

Members were not at all happy with various elements in this case. There was a general feeling that opportunities had been missed to help this sufferer right back at the time when the mother was reporting his sudden change of personality and the dangerous situations she was being subjected to. A carer pointed out 'it seems to me that there was plenty of evidence that Clive was mentally ill and that his mother was in danger'. Yes, others in the group felt that the law could have been used right at the start when Clive subjected his mother to her first ordeal.

The group felt there was a further opportunity to intervene at the time that the mother contacted the psychiatrist asking him for help. It seemed to members that no one was concerned with this mother's needs and safety. When she pleaded for help, she was told by the psychiatrist that if her son didn't bother to turn up for outpatient appointments, he could do nothing. Members agreed with the carer who commented, 'Just not turning up for appointments can indicate there's a problem and this needed to be followed up. This should have been an opportunity for a professional to become involved with this family and find out what was really going on in the home'.

It seemed to members that the psychiatrist did not want to accept his patient's assessment of his own needs and a survivor felt this was a great pity, pointing out that 'Many sufferers realize when they are in hospital that it is the best place to be at that time – it's a smaller and safer world!' 'Yes', someone agreed, 'Clive should have been listened to and he should not have been allowed to discharge himself'.

A carer felt that 'This seems to be another case which demonstrates a lack of understanding of the changing nature of a psychotic illness; there are times when unwell sufferers know what is best for them. This self-insight and knowledge will often disappear during the psychosis, but when it is present then professionals really should listen!'

Someone said at this point, 'This reminds me of the Ben Silcock case. Do you remember the young man who'd been ill with schizophrenia for years and climbed into the lion's den in London Zoo? Apparently, he went to his local hospital and asked to be detained there earlier and was turned away'. 'That's right' another member joined in, 'something about you can't be ill if you're well enough to ask for help, or some such nonsense! I don't know anyone who would climb into a lion's den while they were sane, do you?'

'No, I don't' agreed a carer, 'and it's not that unusual for sufferers to appreciate that they have to be detained for their own good because of this irresistible urge just to keep moving on when they're psychotic. That *is* right, isn't it?' A survivor grinned and agreed that this was absolutely right.

'Yes' someone remarked, 'I once knew a brilliant nurse who had five breakdowns. After the first one, she was always put on a locked ward, at her own request, because that was the only way she could slow down and benefit from treatment; the first time she just kept on running away and everyone spent all their time bringing her back and starting again!'

There was, it seemed plenty of evidence that it is not unusual for sufferers to appreciate in lucid moments of their psychosis that they need to be 'contained' in a safe place and to know that they cannot move on for a while. Clive was denied this facility and members felt that this case study certainly demonstrated a seeming reluctance to use the law to protect a sufferer and his mother (a) early on in his illness when he was clearly very sick and a danger to his mother and (b) later on when he kept requesting he be detained and, finally, (c) after his attempt to kill himself just before he succeeded in this. A survivor summed up how the group felt about this with 'and Clive paid the ultimate price because of this reluctance'.

Malcolm

Members felt that when Malcolm's mother visited the GP's surgery to say she could not take much more of what was happening in her home, the doctor had two courses of action open to her; she could have arranged for a psychiatrist to make a domicillary visit (1), as this provision is particularly appropriate when a sufferer is refusing to see a doctor, or she could, with the co-operation of whichever parent was the nearest relative, have asked Social Services to send an ASW round to the home to assess her patient. The general feeling among the group was that Malcolm should at this point have been returned to the adolescent unit for a re-assessment and appropriate treatment.

Instead, the family's problems escalated to the point where the mother and two younger boys were subjected to a nightmare incident. Members couldn't understand why the ASW and psychiatrist admitted Malcolm to hospital on a voluntary basis; one asked, 'why didn't they use the Mental Health Act and section Malcolm? He was obviously a danger to others, to his family, and he was very ill'. 'Yes, and after all that had gone before, I believe it was obvious that it would be useless to admit him on a voluntary basis. He was no longer co-operating with doctors and he was clearly very ill' added another.

Certainly that was the feeling among the group; that Malcolm would have to be detained at this stage if he was to benefit from treatment. He had been refusing to see his GP or to keep his outpatient appointments and as one carer put it, 'holding a bread knife to his mother's throat was not the behaviour of a sane person or one likely to co-operate with treatment'.

Members pointed out that everyone knew the problem was escalating and that Malcolm's young brothers were living in a atmosphere of fear and threatened violence. There was a strong feeling that this alone should have persuaded professionals to section Malcolm. Indeed, the Code of Practice goes into some detail about the need to consider the circumstances of others living in the home (2). Members didn't feel this had happened.

The group had no doubt that another opportunity to resolve this crisis was missed when Malcolm blackened his mother's eye and she went straight round to seek help from the GP. 'Here was another example that this mother was at risk from Malcolm's outbursts', a carer pointed out, 'and surely it merited a domicillary visit from a psychiatrist at the very least?' Other members agreed that there could be no doubt about this and that this was the sort of situation that this provision was intended to resolve. They were also confident that the law should then have been used to admit Malcolm to hospital to make sure that this time he could have received the treatment he was currently refusing.

Kevin

Members felt it was sad that Kevin and his wife were left to understand that his first manic episode had been caused by his job and that they were given no warning that he might have a recurrence of the illness. As a survivor put it, 'How can anybody understand their illness when this most vital part of the information is denied them?'

A carer agreed that more was called for in the way of explanation and suggested that it would have been helpful if Kevin and his wife could have been told something like 'We're not really sure exactly what it is but many people exhibiting these symptoms do get better with the right help', followed by a brief description about MD and the fact that some people only have one episode of the illness.

Perhaps even more important in this particular case, the group noted that, later on, here was yet another example of a sufferer's medication being stopped after two years of being well, without anyone seeing a need to monitor his progress. Worse, no alarm bells rang when Kevin and his wife sought help so soon afterwards.

Members believed that when Jean and Kevin sought an urgent appointment they shouldn't have been expected to wait a month for this. As a carer pointed out, 'Once again, this was a sufferer seeking help during the critical period before he relapsed into a psychosis. I do wish they'd learn and listen'. In particular, a second carer pointed out that the psychiatrist should have been looking for features which had changed and which were out of character for Kevin – as against looking for 'something wrong' with him and he could have started by asking why the couple had requested an urgent appointment a month earlier and taking note of the fact that Kevin's medication had been stopped two weeks previously!

The group felt that even this belated appointment should have offered an opportunity to admit Kevin to hospital on a voluntary basis to stabilize him once more on the medication. If Kevin hadn't agreed to this, then the doctor should have been alerted to the necessity to keep a watchful eye on his immediate progress. For example, to have mentioned to the GP that there might be a quick deterioration in his patient's condition. Then, they felt, Jean's request for help from the GP might have resulted eventually in a domicillary visit being arranged. Instead, she was given a reply which the LEAP group members have now become familiar with, that is, the doctors could only help if the relapsing sufferer came and asked them for help! A carer pointed out rather wearily that some GPs clearly do not understand something recognized by those responsible for the mental health legislation: that is, that sufferers are unable to seek help for themselves once they become ill.

Not long afterwards, one of the GPs at the local surgery refused Jean's request to come out to Kevin when he was really uptight on the grounds that the problem was really a 'marital dispute'. Members pointed out that the manager of the day centre appeared to make the same implication instead of taking seriously the wife's concern. A survivor's comment seemed to sum up this dangerous sort of assumption with 'Too many times relationships are blamed for people's illnesses when most of the time it is the illness that is affecting the relationship. I wish this was understood.'

The group noted that the missed opportunity to help Kevin a few weeks after he came off the medication, compounded by delays in responding to all the signs of his consequent relapse, turned out to be very bad news insofar as his marriage was concerned. While a survivor was glad to note Jean's understanding of Kevin's illness, a carer felt it a pity that even after the psychiatrist recognized that she 'had been right all along', he and his colleagues did not then take advantage of her expertize and 'take her aboard and work with her' in order to help Kevin with his illness.

Finally, a survivor was glad to note that Jean had her own support system and had no doubt that she was very much in need of this. The marriage of friends of hers, both in the medical profession, had nearly collapsed because of MD but they had eventually worked things out and got back together again. 'I do hope Jean's persistence will pay off in the end', she added.

Kay

Members were very concerned that this young woman was allowed to relapse again after her illness had proved so difficult to treat right through her teens, resulting in years of suffering and despair for sufferer and family. Perhaps understandably, there were strong feelings in the group about this case and one carer had little doubt that she would like to see the law put into force 'as soon as someone comes off their medication. It might sound harsh but that way so many sufferers would not slip through the net needlessly like my son did'. Another carer felt the same way about this; 'This girl had been so ill before, I really do think something should have been done when she announced she was coming off all medication. There was plenty of evidence to show she would deteriorate otherwise'.

A survivor said that she could not agree to this; she was quite sure this would be a premature response. However, she explained, she would have no hesitation about the law being used at the point that the sufferer started to show definite signs of deterioration. 'Kay should have been sectioned "in the interests of her health" at that point', she added (3). A carer was in complete agreement with this, saying 'I wish professionals would focus on the "most appropriate practice" in each case instead of adopting a "least restrictive practice" approach.' This, he felt, could sometimes amount to negligence, when it emphasized patients' rights to forego treatment rather than their right to be well.

Interestingly, and relevant to the last speaker's comment, a member who has had several breakdowns herself gave an example of what might be considered a 'most appropriate practice'; it was her opinion that in circumstances like this the law should allow for medication to be resumed when it has been proved to be so effective as it had been in this case.

No one in the group expressed any reservations about using the law to reinstate this young woman's medication immediately there were signs of deterioration and several members were adamant that 'she should not have been allowed to slide in the first place', as one carer put it. It turned out that these strong feelings hinged on three aspects of this case; (a) that Kay had been so very ill for so long before this particular medication was tried and (b) that she eventually had to be sectioned – but only after two further years of delay and suffering for her and the family and (c) that she had deteriorated by then to the point where the medication no longer helped her very much. Perhaps not surprisingly, this last aspect seemed to the LEAP group members to be the most important factor in this example of a reluctance to use the law 'in the interests of the patient's health'. A carer summed up the general feeling with 'when they eventually used the law it was too late, so Kay's "rights" were not protected whichever way you look at it!'

Debbie

As with several of the cases in this chapter, the LEAP group felt that an opportunity to intervene was missed while this young woman was still prepared to go and see a doctor. Although there was no way of knowing whether or not Debbie had explained, or given away, how she felt, members felt that an experienced GP should have picked up on the fact that something was wrong and that a follow-up after prescribing tablets would have confirmed this. At the very least, the mother's later plea for help must have done so but, as a carer put it, 'this GP believes the myth that the client cannot be helped if they don't ask for help themselves'. 'Yes' a second carer joined in, 'and I find the ignorance of some GPs really scary; I don't know what would have happened to my family if our doctor had responded this way – he was so helpful and arranged for a domicillary visit immediately our son relapsed'.

Another carer felt that Debbie's case was all about a lack of knowledge and understanding of schizophrenic-type illnesses amongst health professionals, and, in particular, the high incidence of them in this young age group (4). He found this very worrying, as did other members. One remarked icily at this point that Debbie would have received more help if she'd had a problem like PMT; 'it's as if everyone's trying to deny serious mental illness exists so each new young sufferer's pain is ignored', she added.

The group could not understand why Social Services had not responded earlier to this mother's requests for help as they are required by law to make arrangements for an individual to be assessed if the nearest relative requests this (5). Could it be that the GP had 'blocked' any previous attempts? At the very least, 'why didn't someone go round and find out for themselves what was going on in this home?' someone asked. Why, indeed?

At this point, the group focused their attention on the mercifully unique feature in this case: a nearest relative driven to the extreme measure of providing indisputable proof of a new sufferer's psychosis. Not surprisingly, members found this quite distressing. As a carer pointed out, 'It seems so sad that the mother, knowing her daughter – and the pain of the previous months – should feel driven to such extreme, covert, lengths. Things were left to go on for far too long – *by people who ought to know better and who are paid to help.*'

Another carer felt angry as well as sad; 'This all comes down to ignorance about schizophrenia, unforgivable in GPs and mental health professionals, and the failure of some GPs to call on other agencies to get involved. They're meant to be the gateway to the mental health services.' She felt nothing would really change until everyone working with serious mental illness became responsible for negligent and uncaring decisions and the suffering these cause. 'Meanwhile,' she added, 'this mother says that no one believed her except for other carers at the NSF group. Why didn't they? What right did any of these professionals have to disbelieve this woman?'

The LEAP group felt this mother's rights had been abused and so had her daughter's rights to expect care and treatment when she became another young victim of a serious mental illness. The only saving grace that members could find in this disturbing case was the heartening determination of the ASW to overcome obstacles put in her way when attempting to arrange Debbie's mental health assessment and the support given her in this by the psychiatrist.

THE WIDER PERSPECTIVE

Members felt there were important issues which cropped up several times in these five cases and also in other cases reported in this book. They went on to discuss these issues:

A need to listen to sufferers when they seek help

Members noted that in four out of these five cases, sufferers sought help in one way or another and none of them received an effective response at that time. Clive finally knew exactly what he needed if he was to survive and he asked for this to be provided. His pleas for help were ignored, with disastrous results.

In Malcolm's case, members felt that it was downhill all the way from the moment that the adolescent unit had discharged him without finding out enough about his problem to help him in any way. This had been the *critical period* – the time before this young man became too ill to understand he needed help – and it had been wasted. 'And once that had happened' a survivor pointed out, 'then professionals had no choice but to use the law, more's the pity!' 'Yes, but they didn't, did they?' exclaimed a carer, 'once this had happened, he and his family were utterly dependent upon professionals who then proceeded to let them down!'

In a way, members found the missed opportunity to heed Kevin when he knew he needed help the most frustrating of all. 'With Clive and Malcolm, doctors just didn't recognize they were really very ill – for some inexplicable reason – but with Kevin the psychiatrist did know he had MD and should have been aware that he had just come off medication too'. 'We don't know whether some of these people just make themselves very inaccessible or if the system lets everyone down and this doctor didn't know Kevin and his wife asked for an early appointment', a carer observed. 'Yes, but he didn't listen and hear what was being said when he did see them, did he?', a survivor pointed out.

Members wondered what Debbie actually said to her GP when she went to see him. There was no way of knowing what might have passed between patient and doctor in this case but members did feel that her co-operation with her mother over this matter could have been better rewarded; 'Surely a doctor would want to follow up to see if the tablets worked or not, or would he just shrug her shoulders if she didn't keep any further appointments she'd been offered?' asked a carer. No one could answer that but at this point the group agreed that it was a great pity that many professionals seemed to be unaware of the *critical period* during which sufferers are still able to recognize that they need help, and accept help.

A carer summed up their feelings with 'when there is so much reluctance to use the law, why don't professionals want to know about the enormous potential to help sufferers during this period before the psychosis sets in?'

A reluctance to use the law

The group felt that four of these five cases studies demonstrated the profound reluctance of some professionals to use the law to protect sufferers from their illness. The most startling example of this was, they felt, Clive's psychiatrist refusing to consider using the law to detain his patient.

Hardly less disturbing, to the minds of the LEAP group members, were the examples of reluctance to use the law in Kay's and Malcolm's cases. Kay proceeded steadily to deteriorate while surrounded by professionals, to the point where the only drug which had controlled her illness was no longer effective. Malcolm was taken into hospital on a voluntary basis having already severed any contact with the system while becoming a real threat to his family.

As for Debbie, the group was at a loss to understand how it could have taken so long for her to be the subject of a mental health assessment. It seemed that not only did professionals not listen to the mother, not one of them explored the situation to the extent of even visiting this home to see for themselves what was happening.

At this point, members pointed out the group had noted other examples of a reluctance to use the law. For example, Kim, Cyril and Dave had each been subjected to two mental health assessments prior to going missing or landing up in prison. Meanwhile, not one measure of protection had been forthcoming as a result of these assessments although each of these individuals was known to have a serious mental illness and people who knew them well were pleading for them to be admitted to hospital. 'When you look at it this way', exclaimed a carer 'you could be forgiven for wondering what some of these professionals were there for, couldn't you?' Yes, and this question conveniently seemed to lead to another issue which concerned the LEAP group.

A need to justify one's actions?

The group noted that questions such as 'how could that professional justify taking that action?' had come up again and again when members had discussed cases in the present chapter and previous ones in this book. They wished they could be assured that those professionals responsible for practice which turned out to be detrimental to a sufferer's future welfare would be expected to justify their actions. They now cited examples of such practice in these five cases, as follows:

1. The response of the psychiatrist to Clive's mother when she asked for help and, later, to her son when he told the doctor what he needed.

2. The response of the GP both times Malcolm's mother sought her help and the decision of the psychiatrist and ASW to admit the young man to hospital on a voluntary basis.

3. The lack of a proper response to Kevin's and Jean's call for urgent help and the psychiatrist's eventual dismissal of their concerns.

4. The lack of any attempt to use the law to protect Kay from a recurrence of her very severe and long-standing illness.

5. The constant refusal of Debbie's doctor to respond to her mother's pleas for help.

Other examples which members cited were:

6. The inactivity of professionals involved in the last two mental health assessments in each of the case studies featuring Kim, Cyril and Dave.

7. The use of Section 2 by ASWs where the law allows for the more appropriate Section 3 to be used, as happened with Sharon and with Sue.

8. The decision by hospital doctors not to convert an inappropriate Section 2 when a patient needed further time and treatment in hospital, as happened, again, with Sharon and with Sue.

A carer summed up the group's feeling about this sort of practice with 'When we're talking about a waste of potential at best, and life or death situations at worse, then I believe professionals should be expected to justify their actions; the conscientious and caring ones would be happy to do this anyway and the practice of those who are less so would surely benefit from this sort of *post mortem* of those cases which suddenly take a turn for the worse'.

It seemed to members that professionals involved with the seriously mentally ill at a time of crisis seem often to work in a vacuum, passing in and out of a case but rarely seeing it through from start to finish. Members thought that this must be very difficult for them at times and that it also led to decisions being made without any feedback being provided at a later date as to how these decisions affected the case in question. The group noted this phenomenon in the first book in this series and they feel this is a grave flaw in the system, forfeiting opportunities to learn from experience what is good and helpful practice and what is less so.

Voluntary organizations

The LEAP group noted that two carers in this chapter have referred to the support they received from organizations such as the MDF and the NSF. The group is very conscious that professionals rarely introduce sufferers and their families to these sorts of resources. They felt this is a great pity as so many of those living with a serious mental illness claim that it is making contact with such organizations that eventually provides them with a means of finding a way forward. A carer summed up his feelings about this, 'It's not as if it costs teams working with the serious mentally ill any time or money to give sufferers and families the relevant telephone numbers at the first opportunity'. 'Yes', agreed a survivor, 'and these sorts of specialist organizations do have an enormous amount of knowledge and expertise at their finger-tips and, goodness knows that sometimes, there's little enough of these precious commodities out there!'

'That's right', a carer agreed, 'some professionals are delighted to take advantage of this specialist knowledge and expertize for their own benefit as well as their clients. I do wish this applied to more of those working with serious mental illness'.

SUMMING UP

In this chapter we have looked at five case studies, each of which focuses on missed opportunities to help sufferers and their families. Members found that where sufferers had been prepared to accept help during the *critical period*, this was not forthcoming. This in turn meant that they became absolutely dependent upon professionals to intervene on their behalf and use the law sooner rather than later, in order to avoid long delays without treatment, waiting for the now inevitable breakdown.

Members found it a cause for grave concern that although the law had, in the end, to be used in the four cases where the individuals survived to this point, not once was it used in time to stop unnecessary suffering and deterioration despite the fact that the Mental Health Act allows for this. They concluded that there may be a pronounced reluctance amongst health professionals to use the law to protect sufferers from the dangers of an untreated psychotic illness.

INFORMATION

(1) Domicillary Visits

In their study of 462 first episodes of schizophrenia, E. C. Johnstone and her colleagues found that 'in particular, knowledge of the availability of domicillary consultations for patients who refuse to visit doctors or hospitals was not widespread' (Johnstone, E. C. *et al.* (1986) the Northwick Park Study of First Episodes of Schizophrenia, Part 1: 'Presentation of the Illness and Problems Relating to Admission', *British Journal of Psychiatry, 148,* 115–120).

The LEAP group members have noted several cases where a domicillary visit by a psychiatrist might well have prevented a threatened crisis when families have sought help from their GP and this has been refused because the sufferer was too ill to ask for help.

(2) Sectioning and the needs of others

Paragraph 2.9 of the *Code of Practice* states that one of the points which those assessing the patient must consider is:'the impact that any future deterioration or lack of improvement would have on relatives or close friends, especially those living with the patient ...' (see p. 6)

(3) A neglected ground for sectioning?

One of the three grounds for compulsory admission to hospital is that it is in the interests of the patient's health. However, there is a widespread misconception that this is not the case. The Foreword of the *Code of Practice* states:

> It has been widely reported that the criteria for admission to hospital under the Act have not been correctly understood by all professionals. In particular, there is said to have been a misconception that patients may only be admitted under the Act if there is a risk to their own or other people's safety. In fact the Act provides for admission in the interests of the patient's health or of his or her safety, or for the protection of other people. This is also clearly spelt out in the new paragraph 2.6 of the Code. (see p. iii and p. 4)

(4) Age group most likely to develop schizophrenia

One in every one hundred of us will develop a schizophrenic illness at some time in our lives but most sufferers (*80 per cent*) are eventually first diagnosed between 16 and 25 years of age.

(5) A nearest relative's request for a mental health assessment

If a nearest relative requests a mental health assessment for a sufferer then Section 13.4 of the Mental Health Act 1983 puts a duty on Social Services departments to arrange for an ASW to assess with a view to deciding whether or not to make an application for the sufferer's admission to hospital.

EXERCISE

Consider a situation in which a government decides that the key factor in cutting down the financial burden and suffering caused by serious mental illness is preventive work. Emphasis is to lie with avoiding long delays caused by sufferers waiting, without treatment, for full-blown crisis situations to erupt. GP practices and mental health teams in the community and in hospitals will be graded and rewarded according to their achievements in normalizing the lives of sufferers and their families. No extra funding or changes in the law are envisaged.

You have been appointed to provide advice and guidance on how this could be achieved. Detail your recommendations.

CHAPTER 8

Mental health assessments
Summing up

In the previous chapters of this book, we have looked at the sort of problems which can occur in getting help when sufferers have lost touch with reality and do not believe they are ill. The LEAP group has studied ten case studies and attempted to determine which factors seem to militate against their chances of being protected from unnecessary damage by their illness.

Let's take a look at the group's findings. Rather than making continual reference to one chapter or another, the names of the individuals concerned have been used and, if required, readers can find the relevant pages in the text under Case Studies in the Index.

'The patient must ask for help' syndrome

When the group analyzed the cases featured in the first book in this series, they found several instances of professionals declining to intervene in a crisis because the sufferer wasn't actively seeking their help. In this second book, members have found examples of professionals giving such a response in half of the ten cases they have analyzed. One doctor repeatedly turned a mother away, despite the fact that no one had attempted to investigate what was happening even when she was reporting atypical, escalating, violence in her daughter.

The LEAP group was perplexed by this sort of reaction from members of a profession which is the acknowledged gateway to the specialist services. Members felt that all health professionals should be aware that sufferers do not recognize they are ill once the psychosis has taken over; hence the old saying, 'You're not mad if you think you are'.

Their refusal to have anything to do with doctors at a time when others are reporting signs of disturbance and dramatic changes should, in itself, be a cause for concern.

More important, perhaps, is that members pointed out that the system provides for just the situation where a patient is refusing to seek help from a GP. The doctor can arrange for a psychiatrist to make a domicillary visit or can consider, with the agreement of the nearest relative, asking Social Services for a mental health assessment to be arranged. The group couldn't understand why some GPs instead chose to turn their backs on patients at a time when their whole future is at risk.

Mental health assessments that lead nowhere

In this book, we have noted quite a few of these abortive mental health assessments, in some cases in quick succession, where professionals have walked away without offering anything although those being assessed were recognized sufferers and those closest to them (family and, frequently, professionals too) were urgently seeking their admission to hospital. As a carer in the group pointed out, ASWs may take up to 14 days to determine whether or not to carry out a section, visiting several times if necessary, yet there was no evidence that this option was considered by any of the ASWs involved in these cases, even where medical recommendations for admission to hospital were already available.

An 'all or nothing' facility?

What really puzzled the LEAP group was the phenomenon whereby mental health assessments had become 'all or nothing' affairs which, on the one hand, could resolve a psychotic crisis by admitting the sufferer into hospital or, on the other, offer nothing more than extra hassle for sufferer and family, with the latter once more left to find their own solution to a nightmare situation.

Not surprisingly, perhaps, members of the LEAP group could not believe that there wasn't a more practical way of facilitating the use of the law to protect a sufferer in need. They felt that some professionals seemed to be 'bending over backwards' to avoid using the law while expecting to provide nothing in its place.

A reluctance to convert inappropriate sections?

The group noted further examples of an apparent reluctance to use the law; this time in the psychiatrists supervising the hospital treatment of Sharon and Sue, whose cases are featured in this book. There was seemingly no attempt made to convert inappropriate 28-day sections to allow the patients time to benefit from their treatment. Instead, one of these doctors attempted to persuade his patient to stay on in hospital after two of her sections expired although she was not well enough to have any insight into her illness. Predictably, she rejected his advice both times.

A 'least restrictive' practice?

Group members were very much aware that the examples quoted above of hospital doctors not converting sections only occurred because of a 'least restrictive' practice approach by some ASWs who seemed to be determined to use Section 2 (rather than the longer six-month Section 3 which allows for the treatment of a diagnosed sufferer) leaving it to hospital teams to convert the section if they felt this was necessary. To do this, the group noted, these ASWs had to ignore both the spirit and letter of the law and also the professional guidance contained in the Code of Practice, which details pointers as to which of these sections is appropriate in which circumstances.

When Sharon's mother challenged this practice the second time her daughter was about to be admitted on a 28-day section, she was given to understand by the ASW that it was up to the psychiatrist to convert the section if he felt this necessary. A member of the LEAP group also had a similar experience when her son was sectioned. In a third case, the ASW actually warned Sue's parents that the section he had applied for would not be adequate for the patient's needs. Perhaps it was not surprising that a member of the group, a survivor herself, was driven to ask 'Do ASWs get brownie points for a "least restrictive" practice or something?' and another member responded with '... ASWs like this do seem to be passing the buck, don't they? Maybe they don't like the responsibilities which go with the power they have?'

Passing the buck?

As we have seen, the group did have further cause to wonder whether some ASWs choose to, or are encouraged to, pass the buck. They found evidence that families are increasingly being urged by ASWs to ring the police in a crisis rather than social workers, if there might be any question of violence. This seemed to members to cover every eventuality; if a psychotic illness is left untreated for long enough, then anything is possible!

Some LEAP group members had recently had this experience with ASWs and it also occurred in cases featured in this book, the most disturbing example leading to a sufferer landing up in prison instead of in hospital. The group found it even more startling in this particular case that the sufferer's parents were advised to call the police if they had further problems by *professionals walking away from mental health assessments without offering any help themselves.* Even if these professionals were so ignorant about the law they worked with to believe they had to witness violent behaviour during the assessment – and this was implied – then they still had a duty not to turn their backs on this situation while there was a chance of the elderly father being assaulted again. Instead they chose to avoid using the mental health legislation and left the family with no option but to call the police when disaster threatened, which was prevented only by the latter's speedy response.

The LEAP group was left to wonder why such professionals have reservations about using the Mental Health Act to restrain a mentally ill sufferer but none, it seems, about leaving it to the police to use the criminal law instead?

A sometimes neglected duty

The group noted that the outcome of one of the cases where the sufferer slipped through the net might have been very different if the nearest relative had been informed of her right to make an application for her daughter Kim's admission to hospital.

As members pointed out, the ASW had a duty to inform the nearest relative of her right to make the application herself and they felt there was little doubt that she would have done this had she been given the opportunity. As it was, her daughter went missing that night. In the Northwick Park Study of First Episodes of Schizophrenia (see under Information in Chapter 2 for details), other families reported that their relative's crisis could have been resolved sooner if they had known about the nearest relative's rights. As it turned out, two members of the LEAP group, too, had not been informed of their rights in similar circumstances. One of them didn't even realize she was the nearest relative until some time after her son's crisis was over. Both of these carers have continued to be shocked by this experience and they pointed out that an ASW who declined to apply for a sufferer's admission to hospital might well be one of those ASWs who are known actively to resist using the law which they are employed to work with. This, they felt, might go some way to explaining why nearest relatives are sometimes kept in ignorance of their right to be 'the alternative applicant'.

The group felt strongly about this matter; how could families take advantage of their legal rights, members asked, if they were not made aware of them? This was a safety net provided by the law and members were concerned that measures should be taken to stop this malpractice, as they saw it, although they were hopeful that only a minority of ASWs would dream of neglecting their duty in this way.

A monopoly of power?

The group was unhappy about the case in which a dying mother's concerns about her son's future turned out to be warranted, perhaps because Cyril was left with no nearest relative to protect his rights? A senior social worker, who was a stranger to the sufferer, overrode the opinions of professionals who did know him. Her decision not to apply for a section had been based on a first, inaccurate, impression of Cyril's personality and on a preoccupation with protecting his rights not to be forced into hospital. Members found this latter preoccupation quite bizarre in someone whose usual role was to decide whether or not sufferers who no longer believed they were ill would benefit from being admitted to hospital. As it was, this sufferer had benefited in the past from treatment in hospital and he stood to lose everything if he was not admitted now. This, in fact, happened.

Members decided that the ASW seemed to have a monopoly of power over her professional colleagues who, unlike her, had considerable knowledge between them of the sufferer.

A basic flaw in the system?

The group was concerned that ASWs so often come to a mental health assessment as a stranger to the case they are assessing and yet may, and sometimes do, override the opinions of other professionals who work with the sufferer on an on-going basis.

To members, this seemed to indicate a basic flaw in the current mental health legislation. In most of the mental health assessments they've come across, the ASWs have not known the sufferers, let alone anything about their everyday lifestyle and relationships. In these circumstances, the group couldn't see how these professionals could judge any changes which had taken place and whether or not they were getting an accurate impression of the usual personality and attitudes of the individual being assessed.

Members cited again the example of the ASW in Cyril's case; she told the GP that the man was clearly abrasive and hostile by nature, which, of course, was the opposite of the truth. He only became abrasive and hostile when he wasn't well; when he was psychotic in fact. His personality changed at such times and this was an indicator, spelt out in his notes, that things were not right with him.

A danger for usually well sufferers when they are relapsing?

The group felt that this last case highlighted their on-going concerns, already discussed in the first book in this series, about the tendency for usually well sufferers with the acute form of schizophrenia to fail to obtain protection from the law. Too often, it seemed to members, strangers to the sufferer and the situation weren't aware of dramatic changes taking place in the sufferer's personality and could see no signs of psychotic behaviour either. Instead they would assume that the individual was usually 'tetchy and suspicious' or 'abrasive and hostile', or, perhaps, overwhelmingly 'effusive'. In Chapter 4 of this book, one cheerful and agreeable survivor in the group mentioned that professionals had found her hostile and domineering during her last breakdown and had assumed this was her normal personality, *despite reports to the contrary from family and friends*. Another survivor pointed out that when individuals like herself were relapsing, 'We won't seem raving mad when we desperately need help; that is, unless they leave us too long and we risk losing everything that matters to us'.

Does it help to be seen to be mad?

Members of LEAP group have highlighted the fact that the law allows for admission to hospital without sufferers needing to be raging mad but in their experience it certainly helps! They gave examples of this from the cases studied in this book. Kevin was sectioned immediately he became really manic in his first two episodes of his illness but later, even though he now had a diagnosis of MD, he wasn't admitted when he desperately needed medication; his behaviour was more controlled and he wasn't running amok. The same thing happened with Kim; she was admitted to hospital whenever she was running wild but was left to become very ill – and perhaps to perish – when her psychosis was more contained, even though she had recently taken two overdoses in one week. Similarly, Clive was considered to be too sane to need protecting from himself; his torment was not so obvious to others, it seemed. Members felt this was one of the main reasons why the most seriously deluded sufferers were often refused the protection of the law; they were able to 'contain their madness' as two of the survivors in LEAP group had reported about themselves, or they could be regarded as 'play-acting' as happened with Sue.

The group could find no answer to this phenomenon, except urging everyone involved in crisis work to be aware that it is a common one and that it will be missed *unless the opinions and evidence of those closest to the sufferer are heeded.* It is they who will know if the sufferer has changed dramatically and is deteriorating and, as we have seen, the Mental Health Act allows for admission to hospital 'in the interests of the patient's health'. Members know of cases where a relapse has been arrested in a matter of days, allowing the suffer to get on with their life again after a small hiccup, rather than having to endure a protracted period of misery and potential disaster.

A question of attitudes?

The LEAP group has looked at where things can go wrong with trying to get help in a crisis, starting with the early signs of a relapse through to sufferers slipping through the net even at a late stage in a psychotic episode. Members feel that the sort of problems we have noted in this book tend to have more to do with deep-seated attitudes towards psychotic illness and the use of the law than with an increasing scarcity of resources. Because of this, they believe it is quite possible that any future legislation may not dramatically influence the precariousness of living with a serious mental illness except, perhaps, for the most severely ill sufferers and their families. With this in mind, the group have decided to conclude this summing up of their findings with a plea for a concerted effort by everyone concerned to find a new way forward, perhaps on the lines of the proposal below?

The potential for 'working in partnership'

It has been clear for a long time now that there is a reluctance among professionals working with serious mental illness to use the law. Not surprisingly, this reluctance is more than matched by the keen dread of sufferers and their families of having to endure yet one more psychotic crisis. This seems to the LEAP group to be the one common ground shared by everyone involved with psychotic illness; a strong desire to avoid the delays and damage associated with crisis situations and the last minute trauma-ridden admissions to hospital which presently accompany them.

The LEAP group believes that this can all change when service providers appreciate the potential of sufferers and those closest to them to take control of their own lives and when they facilitate this by working in partnership with them. Members feel that the time has come for them to be 'welcomed aboard' by the professionals who pass through the sufferer's life at different times. This way, the expertize of those closest to the sufferer would not be wasted as it so often is at present and something like real continuity of care could be achieved instead of the often abortive attempts at trying a new approach by a succession of newcomers who then move on. Sufferers, like the rest of us, usually choose to live with those closest to them and, because of this, those whom the system recognizes as carers usually know what matters most to sufferers *when they are well* and are also quick to note the first subtle signs of things going wrong, Few, if any, professionals have the opportunity to get to know their clients or patients this well, nor, increasingly, do they have the opportunity to stay with them for any reasonable length of time either.

One carer has put it this way: she would like professionals to realize that sufferers and carers choose to be with each other during the good times and to appreciate that many of them do just that without being a burden to the system. It is only when a threatened relapse changes all that overnight that both sufferer and carer need professionals to intervene and stop the rot. This, she feels, will only happen if there is trust and respect between carers and professionals and if the system listens and provides help while the sufferer can still accept this.

The LEAP group believes that this sort of partnership between professionals and families, particularly with sufferers, who are now beginning to make a strong case for having a say in their treatment programmes and for using *advance directives* to make clear what they want to happen if they become ill and out of touch with reality, will lead to professionals finding their work much more rewarding and worthwhile. Members hope they will want to give it a try!

Glossary

The term serious (or severe) mental illness refers to those conditions which can cause sufferers to become psychotic, so losing touch with reality. The most common of these are schizophrenia and manic depression. The following brief, and inevitably over-simplified, definitions may help readers who are not well acquainted with these illnesses.

MANIC DEPRESSION (MD)

This illness is an 'affective' disorder with severe mood swings. The individual may at any one time experience profound depression or mania. Sufferers describe their depressive episodes as being enveloped by a dark cloud but many experience a manic episode as being exciting and euphoric; a brilliant and creative phase. That is, until their 'high' escalates out of control and they slip into a psychosis, at which point the euphoria can become a disaster, once more disrupting the sufferer's life.

Mania begins with a build-up of symptoms, including a general **speeding up of movement and speech; a lack of sleep; enhanced creativity and awareness; an inflated self-confidence,** alongside increasing **irritability and impatience with others.** There is often **pressure of speech** (a compulsive need to talk continuously); **flight of ideas** (an inability to follow through one line of thought or idea); **a disturbing loss of judgement** (putting the individual very much at risk); lots of grand ideas, including a **preoccupation with spending money** and a **lack of inhibition** which, in some cases, can lead to uncharacteristic **promiscuity.** At this stage of a manic episode, it is not uncommon for the sufferer to experience some of the psychotic symptoms listed under 'acute' schizophrenia below.

The depressive episodes in MD may be seen as the 'down' and reverse side of mania, and the sufferer's experience may include a general **slowing down of movement and speech; a lack of energy and motivation; increased inhibition; impaired concentration and ability to undertake the simplest tasks; distorted feelings of guilt and self-loathing; anxiety and agitation and morbid thoughts of death**, and, worse, **suicidal ideas.** Severe depression can escalate into a psychosis with hallucinations and delusions, but this is not so common as with mania.

These days, the excesses of MD can usually be controlled by one of the various mood-stabilizing drugs now available and the prognosis can be good. However, some individuals suffer distressing side-effects and one of these can be a dampening down of their often considerable creative ability which may make them reluctant to comply with treatment.

SCHIZOPHRENIA

The 'acute' form of schizophrenia is characterized by a cluster of so-called 'positive' symptoms and these include (a) **hallucinations,** when any of, or all, five senses may play tricks on the individual, the most common being the 'hearing of voices', (b) **delusions,** when all sorts of incredible ideas become fixed beliefs in the individual's mind and impervious to any reasoned argument. The most distressing and damaging of these can be the **paranoia** which convinces sufferers that other people – usually those who matter most to them – are plotting against them, and (c) **thought disturbance** with sufferers having all sorts of bizarre experiences such as finding their thoughts have taken on a life of their own, leading to ideas that their minds have been taken over by an outside source. These then are examples of the sort of experiences we call 'positive' symptoms, which make up the main part of an 'acute' schizophrenic illness. They are usually controlled by anti-psychotic medication but some 'acute' sufferers relapse into further psychotic episodes, particularly if they cut down or discontinue their medication. Because of this, there is an urgent need for a preventive approach to the handling of this illness.

The *chronic* form of schizophrenia is characterized by an ongoing and persistent cluster of 'negative' symptoms (so called because they take something away from the individual's original personality) which are disabling and in many ways quite different to those of acute schizophrenia. These include severe **lethargy**; profound **apathy; poverty of speech**, precluding any real ability to initiate conversation or indulge in what we know as 'small talk', **impaired concentration** making it difficult to even read a few lines of a newspaper; **emotional blunting**, in which sufferers may demonstrate no interest in or emotions about those closest to them and a general flatness in a 'grey' world where they feel no anticipation or excitement, with none of the highs and lows most of us experience in everyday life. All this can be socially crippling and amount to severe impairment and a change in personality which can make sufferers, and those closest to them, feel they have lost the person they once knew.

Despite the differences in the 'acute' and 'chronic' forms of the illness, there is an overlap between them. 'Acute' sufferers can experience some of these 'negative' symptoms following a breakdown and, tragically, some slip into the chronic form of the illness after one breakdown too many. Similarly, many 'chronic' sufferers can relapse into acute episodes of the illness, particularly if they are not protected by 'maintenance' medication.

General Glossary

Approved Social Worker (ASW): a professional, without medical training, who is qualified to work with the mental health law and to determine whether or not to make application for a sufferer's compulsory admission to hospital (given the required medical recommendations are available).

Clinical Psychologist: a professional who can help sufferers cope with their symptoms, with tools such as cognitive therapy.

Community Psychiatric Nurse (CPN): a professional who provides ongoing support and care for the patient in the community. Also monitors medication and gives injections.

Critical Period: the limited time before a breakdown when sufferers realize they are relapsing and in need of help.

Delusion: a firmly held belief which has no basis in reality.

Family Theories: popular theories from the 1960s and 1970s, now discredited, which blamed families for their relative's schizophrenic illness.

Depot Injection: an injection into the muscle tissue of neuroleptic medication which is then slowly released, lasting anything from one to four weeks.

Genetic Risk: while we all have a one per cent chance of becoming schizophrenic at some time during our lives, research points to a raised risk in individuals with relatives who are sufferers; with one parent or brother or sister – 10 per cent; with two parents – 30 per cent; with an identical twin – 45 per cent.

GP: a doctor providing general medical treatment and care within the community who is the 'gateway' to all psychiatric services. Can also recommend their patient's compulsory admission to hospital.

Hallucination: an altered or abnormal perception affecting one's hearing, vision, taste, smell or touch. The most common type is auditory – the hearing of 'voices' for which there is no rational explanation.

Labelling Theory: popular theory originating from the 1960s claiming that a diagnosis of mental illness is little more than a stigmatized label put on someone who is 'deviant'. Consequently, professionals (rather than sufferers and their families) still tend to avoid acknowledging psychotic illness.

Mental Health Assessment: an assessment by an ASW and doctor(s) to determine whether or not someone mentally ill needs to be compulsorily admitted to hospital.

Nearest Relative: defined by the law and often the elder of a sufferer's parents or the spouse. Has certain rights, including that of making application for the individual's compulsory admission to hospital (given the required medical recommendations are available) if an ASW declines to do this.

Neuroleptic Medication: the drugs which have been used since the early 1950s to control psychotic symptoms. New ones have become available during the 1990s, helping some of those unaffected by the original medication.

Occupational Therapist: a professional who works with individual or groups of patients in hospital or in the community, facilitating rehabilitation and supporting them in adapting to an appropriate lifestyle.

Personality Disorder: a little understood blanket term and an unwelcome label received by many individuals with a serious mental illness before their psychotic behaviour is properly understood and diagnosed.

Police: often involved in crisis work; can use Section 136 of the Mental Health Act, 1983, to take someone from a public area to a 'safe place' such as hospital or police station if they appear to be seriously mentally ill, so that an ASW can arrange a mental health assessment.

Psychiatrist: a specialist doctor in charge of patients' psychiatric treatment in hospital and in the community. Can also recommend their compulsory admission to hospital.

Psychiatric Nurse: a professional who can work within a hospital, a formal hostel or the community, providing nursing care and support and the monitoring/administration of medication. See also CPN.

Psychosis: a condition in which sufferers lose touch with reality and have no recognition of the fact that they are mentally ill and in need of help. When this happens it usually means that treatment cannot be administered unless professionals use the mental health law to admit the individual to hospital.

Sectioning: the use of the law to compulsorily admit someone with a mental illness to hospital.

Serious Mental Illness: conditions such as manic depression and schizophrenia which can cause the individual to lose touch with reality, ie, to become psychotic.

Social Worker: a professional concerned with arranging accommodation for patients and assessing, as appropriate, other practical needs. May provide support for sufferers in the community and/or their families, usually on a short-term basis. See also ASW.

Further Reading

Department of Health and Welsh Office (1993) *Code of Practice: Mental Health Act 1983*: HMSO. Available from HMSO, PO Box 276, London SW8 5DT (tel 0171 873 9090).

The Code of Practice should really be mandatory reading for all professionals who work with the seriously mentally ill or, at the very least, be made readily available for everyone at the work place. Also useful for families caught up in a crisis situation which may call for resort to the law.

Copeland, M. E. (1994) *Living with Depression and Manic Depression*. Harbinger Publications Incorporated.

Beautifully presented and useful book from the USA by an MD sufferer and campaigner. She outlines a day-by-day self-management approach to coping with this type of illness (which could perhaps best be described as 'working in partnership' with professionals and a selected group of supporters). Includes advice on drawing up advance directives, or 'living wills', and generally brings a new meaning to the words 'self-determination'.

Greer, C. and Wing, J. (1988) *Schizophrenia at Home*. National Schizophrenia Fellowship (see under Useful Addresses).

This is the second edition of a book first published in 1974 and it clearly demonstrates that little changes for families trying to cope with serious mental illness. The first edition represented an innovative decision to reveal the experiences of relatives of sufferers and to present these in a 'plain and unvarnished way'. Two decades later the book is still a valuable source of information.

Howe, G. (1991) *The Reality of Schizophrenia*. London: Faber & Faber.

By the present author, this book sets out to explain the historical perspective and content of all the 'muddled thinking', as she puts it, surrounding schizophrenia. In doing this, it also covers most of the important aspects of coping with the illness.

Howe, G. (1997) *Serious Mental Illness: A Family Affair*. London: Sheldon Press.

This book, by the present author, is written to help lay-people understand conditions such as manic depression and schizophrenia. In particular, it is for sufferers and families trying to cope with this type of illness. It covers practical issues, getting the best from the system, coping in a crisis and, perhaps most importantly, how to avoid a crisis!

Howe, G.(1995) *Working with Schizophrenia: A Needs Based Approach.* London: Jessica Kingsley Publishers.

This book was written by the present author, with contributions from 12 sufferers and carers and several professional colleagues. Primarily written for individuals working with this illness, it has received an accolade of enthusiastic reviews in the relevant professional journals.

Kuipers, L. and Bebbington, P. (2nd edition, 1997) *Living With Mental Illness.* London: Souvenir Press Ltd. (Human Horizons Series).

Written by a psychologist and psychiatrist for relatives of the mentally ill; families should find it informative and helpful.

Manic Depression Fellowship (1995) *Inside Out: A Guide to Self Management of Manic Depression.* Produced and published by Manic Depression Fellowship (see under Useful Addresses).

This innovative and valuable booklet reflects the enthusiasm among the membership of MDF for a self-management approach to coping with this illness, largely inspired by the work of Mary Ellen Copeland (see above).

Manic Depression Fellowship (1997) *A Balancing Act.* Produced and published by Manic Depression Fellowship (see under Useful Addresses).

An extremely useful book. To quote MDF's *Pendulum*, 'it is aimed at the people who live alongside and help those who have a diagnosis of MD. It includes techniques and strategies which carers have found helpful'

Varma, V. (1997) *Managing Manic Depressive Disorders.* London: Jessica Kingsley Publishers.

Provides useful information and analysis for people who are concerned with manic depressives. Discusses the possibilities of treatment and self-management.

Useful Addresses

Concern for the Mentally Ill
30 Arkwright Road
London NW3 6BH
Fax: 0181 444 5269
A registered charity 'to promote and protect the welfare of the mentally disordered' and to provide a united voice for professionals involved in the care, treatment and rehabilitation of mentally vulnerable people.

Depression Alliance
35 Westminster Bridge Road
London SE1 7JB
Tel: 0171 633 0557
Concerned with helping sufferers and their families to cope with a depressive illness. Provides advice and information about the illness and seeks to education public opinion. Quarterly newsletter, *A Single Step*.

Making Space
46 Allen Street
Warrington
Cheshire WA2 7JB
Tel: 0925 571 680
Concerned with assisting sufferers and families in the North of England and promoting community care facilities and education.

Manic Depression Fellowship (MDF)
8–10 High Street
Kingston-upon-Thames
Surrey KT1 1EY
Tel: 0181 974 6550
Offers advice and support to those having to cope with MD, frequent open meetings and local self-help groups. Also involved in campaigning and promoting better services. Quarterly journal, *Pendulum*.

National Schizophrenia Fellowship (NSF)

18 Castle Street
Kingston-upon-Thames
Surrey KT1 1SS
Tel: 0181 547 3937

Concerned with helping those affected by serious mental illness, while providing community services and promoting education and knowledge. Conferences and training days and local self-help groups throughout the country. Addresses and telephone numbers of regional offices can be obtained from head office. Quarterly newsletter, *NSF Today*. Highly recommended helpline: 0181 974 6814 (10am–3pm weekdays).

SANE

199–205 Old Marylebone Road
London NW1 5QP
Tel: 071 724 6520

Concerned with research, campaigning and promoting knowledge about serious mental illness. Pioneering research at SANE's Prince of Wales International Centre in Oxford. Occasional newsletter, *Sanetalk*. SANE Helpline: 0171 724 8000 (afternoons, evenings and weekends).

Subject Index

Accident, walking away
    from 17
Advance directives 140
Anti-depressants
    see Medication
Anti-psychotic drugs
    see Medication
ASWs
    and a flaw in the
        system? 137
    Cyril's case 52–5,
        58–60, 62
    Debbie's case 116,
        125
    Kim's case 19–22, 27,
        28, 30–3
    Dave's case 73–4, 83
    duties 28, 31–2, 136
    Kevin's case 112
    Malcolm's case 111,
        119
    powers 66, 68, 136–7
    Sharon's case
    Sue's case 90–9, 97–9,
        104

Behaviour and
    personality changes
    61, 64, 66, 68, 73,
    109, 137–8
Bystanders and
    onlookers, 17

Cannabis, see street drugs
Care plan 46, 99, 105
Care programme 105
Carers 73–5, 88–107

and community care
    105
as providers of com-
    munity care 105
as victims 46–7,
    73–75, 104,
    103–4, 108–10,
    118, 120, 125
not being listened to
    38–41, 44, 73–4,
    78, 92, 98, 101,
    110–11, 113, 115,
    119, 120–2,
    124–7
quality of life 93, 95,
    100
their fears 52–3,
    73–4, 89, 90, 104,
    115–17
see also Nearest relative
Case studies 9 –10
    Clive 109–10
    Cyril 52–7
    Dave 71–5
    Debbie 115–17
    Kay 114–15
    Kevin 112–14
    Kim 18–23
    Malcolm 110–12
    Sharon 36–40
    Sue 88–94
Casualty department 21,
    26
Children, needs of and
    rights 111, 119, 120
Civil rights 16, 56,
    61–2, 83, 85, 123,
    125
Clinging relationship 62,
    63, 69
Code of Practice, 16, 28,
    49, 50, 69, 86, 97,
    98, 106–7, 120,
    130, 134

College 18, 20, 36–38,
    42–4
Community care 84
    carers providing 105
    part-time 94, 100
Community psychiatric
    nurse see CPN
Continuity of care 63,
    77, 94, 100–2, 105,
    139
CPNs 14, 67, 102
    Cyril's case 52–5,
        58–60, 62
    Dave's case 73–5, 78,
        80, 85
    Kay's case 114
    Kim's case 20–3,
        25–8,
    Sharon's case 38, 39,
        43
    Sue's case 93–4, 102
Criminal system 71, 80,
    81, 83, 84, 86, 97
Critical period 13, 14,
    109, 110, 117, 118,
    121, 125–6, 129

Day centre/drop-in 20,
    58, 112, 113, 114,
    115, 121
Department of Health
    29, 105
Deterioration 95, 115,
    122, 123
Diabetes, analogy with
    schizophrenia 64, 7
Domicillary visit 72, 96,
    106, 119, 120–21,
    124, 130, 133

'Enemy', the 17
Exercises, at end of
    chapters 35, 51, 70,
    87, 108, 131

Family theories of
schizophrenia 47,
50, 63, 69, 103
Families, *see* carers

GPs
Clive's case 109, 110
Cyril's case 54–6, 59,
61, 66
Dave's case 71–4,
76–78, 80
Debbie's case 115–17,
123–4, 126
Kevin's case 112, 113,
121,
Kim's case 19, 22, 24,
25, 27
Malcolm's case 111,
119, 120
Sharon's case 36, 41,
45
Sue's case 89, 103

Homelessness 57, 60, 61,
62
Hospital
admission to 15, 19,
20, 37, 39, 75, 91,
93, 104, 110–13,
117, 136
discharge from 75, 88,
93, 99, 103, 113,
117
discharging oneself
38–9, 46, 110–11
Housing department 53,
55, 56, 60

Insight 40, 77

Landlord 20–3, 26, 28,
30
Law, mental health, 67,
76, 79–80, 91, 93,
95, 98, 99
attitudes towards 139

basic flaw 137
for protection 48–9,
109, 138
grounds for using,
14–16, 29, 95,
130
not in the spirit of
27–8, 134
'least restrictive'
practice 33, 36–37,
40, 42–5, 47–9,
51, 123, 127–8,
134–5
missed opportunities
to use 110, 119,
120, 123, 129
reluctance to use
16–17, 23, 29, 71,
80, 109, 117, 119,
125–7, 129, 134,
139
see also Sectioning
Lithium – *see* mood
stabilizers under
Medication

'Mad' behaviour,
advantages of 8, 31,
64, 138
Manic depression (MD)
definition, 141–2
Manic Depression
Fellowship 114,
128, 148
'Marital dispute' 113,
121
Marriage 72, 77, 112,
113, 122
MD, *see* manic depression
Medication 14, 19, 26,
89, 99, 193–4, 100,
111
anti-depressants 19,
36

anti-psychotic/neuro-
leptic drugs 14, 19,
92, 110, 114
coming off, 96,
113–15, 121, 125
depot injections 20,
21, 25, 53, 58, 59,
63, 75
mood stabilizers 37,
41, 43, 46, 112
persevering with 26,
42, 77
role of 76–7, 142
side effects 77, 78,
142
Mental Health Act 1983,
see Law.
see also Mental health
assessments,
sectioning and
sections
Mental health
assessments carried
out 19, 20, 21, 22,
37–9, 54–6, 73–4,
91, 111–13, 115,
117
resolving nothing 27,
30, 33, 127,
133–4
see also Law,
Sectioning, and
Sections
Message, for
professionals 10
Misconception,
widespread, 16, 29,
33–4, 130
'Missing' 90–1, 96, 98

National Schizophrenia
Fellowship 116,
125, 128, 149
Nearest relative

definition, 34–5
need for 66
rights as alternative
    applicant 28, 31–5,
    90, 101, 107, 116,
    124–5, 131,
    135–6
Neuroleptic drugs, see
    Medication

Occupational therapist,
    definition 144
Overdose 21–23, 26,
    110

'Passing the buck' 48–9,
    76, 82–4, 97, 135
Parents, see carers
'Patient has to ask for
    help' syndrome 19,
    20, 89–90, 110,
    113, 116, 132
Personality changes
    see Behaviour/
    personality changes
Personality clash 74
Physical abuse
'Play-acting' 92
Police 74–5, 79, 80–1,
    84, 91, 97, 107,
    112
    and 'call them' 83, 97,
    116, 135
    reputation of 75, 80,
    86
    role of 82, 83, 85
Prison 75, 76, 81, 86
Professionals,
    message for 10
    misconception, 16, 29,
    33–4, 130
    training 45, 63,
    68–70
Psychiatrists

Clive's case 109, 110,
    118, 126
Cyril's case 54, 56, 59,
    67
Dave's case 72–5, 78
Kay's case 114–15
Kevin's case 112–13,
    122, 125
Kim's case 19, 20, 22,
    24, 25, 29
Malcolm's case 111,
    119
Sharon's case 37–9,
    43–6
Sue's case 90–100
Psychologist, clinical,
    definition 143
Psychosis 129
    definition 13
Psychotic crisis 13,
    103–4
Relatives, see Carers,
    see also Nearest relative
Responsibility issues 82,
    124, 127–8

SANE 149
Scapegoating 65
Schizophrenia
    definition 142–3
    family theories 47, 50,
    63
    incidence of 131
    age at diagnosis 131
Sectioning a 'least
    restrictive practice'
    33, 36–7, 40,
    42–45, 47–9, 51,
    123, 128, 134–5
    carried out 19, 20,
    37–9, 117
    definition 15
    grounds for, 14–16,
    29, 95, 130

'not carried out' 21,
    22, 54–56, 73–74,
    110, 111, 112
    see also ASWs, Law,
    Mental health
    assessments, Mental
    Health Act,
    Sections
Sections
    definition 15
    most appropriate
    38–9, 43, 48, 134,
    up to14 days grace,
    27, 30, 133
    see also ASWs, Law,
    Mental health
    assessments, Mental
    Health Act,
    Sectioning
Serious mental illness
    definition 13
Social workers 20, 25,
    56–7, 65, 67–8,
    111
    see also ASWs
Social network 57, 58,
    68
Street drugs 18, 19, 22,
    24
Sufferers, a need to be
    listened to 13, 14,
    109, 110, 117, 118,
    121, 125–6, 129

Urgency, a need for,
    63–4, 113, 121
Users, see Sufferers

Voluntary organizations
    128, 129

Working in partnership
    94, 100, 101, 102,
    139

Name Index

Sue, 'carers' experience' case study, 88–94

Tyler, Mary 86

Wyatt, R.J. 34

Bleuler, M. 106

Clive, 'ignoring sufferer's pleas' case study 109–10

Crow, T.J. 34

Cyril, 'refusal to section' case study 52–7

Dave, 'into the wrong system' case study, 71–5

Debbie, 'ignoring mother's pleas' case study, 115–17

Howe, G. 11, 50, 69

Johnstone, E.C. 35, 106, 130

Kay, 'a responsibility to intervene' case study 114–15

Kety, S. 70

Kevin, 'a delayed response' case study 112–14

Kim, 'a responsibility to intervene' case study 18–23

Malcolm, 'denial of illness' case study 110–12

Sharon, 'a least restrictive practice' case study 36–40